THE
QUILTING
AND
PATCHWORK
PROJECT BOOK

20 SIMPLE STEP-BY-STEP PROJECTS

KATHERINE GUERRIER

THE
APPLE
PRESS

A QUINTET BOOK

Published by The Apple Press
6 Blundell Street
London N7 9BH

ISBN 1–85076–481–6

This book was designed and produced by
Quintet Publishing Limited
6 Blundell Street
London N7 9BH

Creative Director: Richard Dewing
Project Editor: Stefanie Foster
Designer: Nicky Chapman
Editor: Anne Neville
Photographer: Ian Howes

Typeset in Great Britain by
Central Southern Typesetters, Eastbourne
Manufactured in Singapore by Eray Scan Pte Ltd
Printed in Singapore by
Star Standard Industries Private Ltd

CONTENTS

INTRODUCTION

The idea of making something both beautiful and useful from materials which may otherwise be discarded, or which cost little, is very appealing, especially in today's climate of conservation and recycling. Many of the projects in this book need only small amounts of fabric which, if you are already engaged in dressmaking or other sewing projects, you may have already.

Suitable fabrics for patchwork include pure cotton in dress- or light furnishing-weight, needlecord, lawn, poplin or polycotton. Stretch or knit fabrics are not suitable for patchwork. Start a collection of fabrics in colours and prints that you like and will enjoy using. Whenever I see a likely looking fabric, I buy a quarter or half-yard (metre) piece to add to mine. There are many fabric and notions firms which supply materials and equipment specifically for the quilt-maker, and the range of colours and prints available is almost unlimited. Look in the small ads of the sewing and patchwork magazines; many offer samples for mail order. Other sources are the remnant boxes in department stores and at market stalls. If

using old garments, cut away worn or faded parts. All fabrics should be washed and ironed before use to test for shrinkage and how fast the dye is.

Batting (wadding) is the padding which is used as an interlining between the top

of a quilt and the back. The projects in this book use mainly the polyester batting, in either 2–oz or 4–oz weight as this is the most economical and practical. More specific details are given with each project.

EQUIPMENT FOR CUTTING AND SEWING

Most of the necessary equipment required is the same as that for dressmaking with one or two additions.

SCISSORS

Keep one pair of sharp scissors for cutting out fabric only, and another pair especially for paper. A pair of fine embroidery scissors is useful for snipping threads and trimming seam allowances.

PINS

Choose good-quality pins and discard any

that become rusty. The glass-headed variety are easier to pick up. Keep them in a pin-cushion rather than a tin, which will make them easier to retrieve if you drop them. For delicate fabrics, wedding-dress pins are long and fine.

NEEDLES

A variety of sizes is useful. For general hand sewing use Sharps number 8 or 9, which are fine and long enough to take three or four stitches at a time. For hand quilting use Betweens size 10. (The higher

the number the smaller is the needle.)

THREAD

You will need a collection of threads for hand and machine sewing. As with fabrics, start a collection of different colours. When sewing patchwork, try to match the thread to the fabric as far as possible. A slightly darker thread than fabric will sometimes blend better when colour values are being combined. Quilting thread is thicker than machine thread and better for hand sewing.

THIMBLE

This is essential if you plan to hand stitch and especially so for quilting by hand. There are various types available; choose one which is comfortable. For general hand sewing I prefer the leather ones.

WAX

This will prevent knotting and strengthen the thread when hand stitching.

TAPE MEASURE

An essential item in any workbox, most now have both imperial and metric measurements.

UNPICKER (SEAM RIPPER)

This is more efficient than scissors for unpicking small stitches.

IRON

Patches and seams must be well pressed, so a good steam iron or a dry iron and mist sprayer is essential.

SEWING MACHINE

This will speed up the process of construction and is necessary for some projects.

FABRIC MARKER

Choose one with which you can get a fine line on the fabric. The fading type of felt-tip marker is a good choice. The line will fade after 24 hours.

QUILTER'S QUARTER

The seam allowance used in patchwork is ¼ in (6 mm) so a quilter's quarter – a ruler with ¼ in (6 mm) sides all round – is a useful tool both for checking these and making templates.

ROTARY CUTTING SET

Three items make up the rotary cutting set: the cutter itself which is a circular blade set in handle, the cutting board – this is made of "self-healing" material which does not score and is marked out in a grid, and the broad ruler which is made of thick, clear plastic and is also marked with a grid. This equipment saves time when cutting out fabrics, especially with the simple shapes such as strips, squares, rectangles and triangles. Up to six layers of fabric can be cut together.

USING THE ROTARY CUTTER

The circular blade is very sharp so always be sure to put the guard on when it is not in use. To prepare the fabric, fold or stack four to six layers together with raw edges even and the straight grain aligned. Steam press. Place them on the cutting board and first straighten one edge of the fabrics by holding the ruler down firmly near the edge of the stack and running the cutter along the ruler's edge. Hold the blade towards the ruler and cut away from you. Now line up this straight edge with one of the grid lines on either the board or the ruler and cut the required widths and lengths. Remember when cutting to include seam allowances of ¼ in (6 mm) on each side of the patches or strips, eg. for a finished square of 4 in (10.2 cm) cut 4½ in (11.4 cm) squares.

Before starting on a project with the

Using a rotary cutter.

rotary cutter, practise with scrap fabric to learn the technique. Keep the blade pressing against the ruler (it has a tendency to veer outwards and away at first) and go slowly. Hold the ruler firmly. For certain projects the rotary cutter can more than halve the time spent preparing fabrics, so it is worth the small amount of practice required to learn the technique.

EQUIPMENT FOR DESIGNING

Equipment for the workroom.

CARTRIDGE PAPER
This is needed for papers used in the "English Method", but used envelopes or paper of a similar weight will do just as well.

GRAPH PAPER
Squared graph paper will give accurate right angles. Isometric graph paper is marked out in triangles and can be used for making templates for hexagons and diamonds of any size.

COLOURED PENCILS AND FELT-TIP PENS
It is always useful to try out different colour combinations at the planning and designing stage, so keep a selection of different colours.

AN ACCURATE RULER
This is necessary for drawing and measuring templates.

TRACING PAPER, GLUE AND STIFF CARD OR TEMPLATE PLASTIC
Templates can be made from any of these materials.

TECHNIQUES

Where a particular technique is used in several of the projects it is included in this section, but where a technique is specific to one project only (as for the Folded Star Stationery Folder) it appears with the project instructions.

AMERICAN BLOCK PATCHWORK

American block patchwork uses a repeated unit of shapes which, when put together, form the basis of a quilt design. The blocks can be purely patchwork, appliqué, quilting or a combination. It is said that this method of making a quilt-top was evolved when American quilt-makers had little space in which to work and each block was made individually on the lap and stacked away until enough were completed to be stitched together. This avoided the inconvenience of having an ever-growing sheet of patchwork in the limited space available. When blocks are placed edge to edge, interesting secondary designs appear, often merging the separate blocks into a complex overall design.

PATCHWORK BLOCKS

There are many patchwork or "pieced" blocks, often with individual names such as Bear's Paw or Sherman's March. Each block requires one or more templates – the master pattern pieces from which the fabric patches are cut. Patches are placed with right sides of the fabric together and sewn with a small running-stitch by hand or machine.

MAKING THE TEMPLATES

Rather than tracing templates from books and magazines, it is far more versatile and just as easy to make your own. This will give you the freedom to adapt traditional block designs and enable you to change the size of a block, add a border where appropriate and combine features from more than one design.

American Star Block.

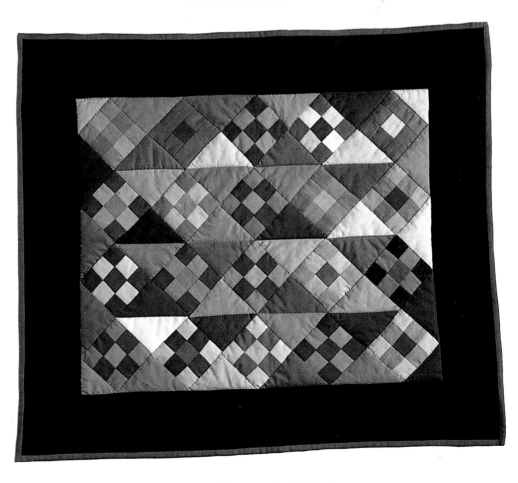

This quilt combines two simple blocks.

In order to demonstrate the technique a simple Star Block is used. First decide what size you want to make your block: 12 in (30.5 cm), 14 in (35.6 cm) or 16 in (40.6 cm) square are all convenient sizes to use, both for smaller items such as bags or pillows, or large ones such as a quilt. Draw the block full size on squared graph paper (see diagrams). This will ensure accuracy on 90 degree angles. Identify how many different templates are needed, in this case three – one square and two triangles in different sizes.

Cut one of each from your drawing and glue them onto stiff card. When cutting out the fabric patches, a seam allowance of ¼ in (6 mm) must be added. If you plan to machine piece your blocks, add the seam allowance to all sides of each template before cutting out the card. If you plan to hand piece, you may prefer to add the seam allowance as you cut the fabric. This means that you can draw round the template onto the fabric to give a guideline for hand sewing. When making templates, make sure they are drawn and cut out accurately so that the patchwork block will fit together.

CUTTING OUT THE PATCHES

Wash and iron the fabrics and smooth them out on a flat surface, wrong side up. Note the fabric grain lines onto the templates. These lines should run parallel wih the sides of the block wherever possible. Mark accurately round the template onto the fabric with a marker pen holding the template wrong side up. This will prevent cutting a mirror-image patch where the shape is non-reversible. If you are to add the seam allowance as you cut (ie, for a hand-pieced block), remember to leave enough space between patches, that is, two seam allowance widths (½ in/1.2 cm). If templates have already had the seam allowance added (ie, for a machine-pieced block), they can be placed edge to edge.

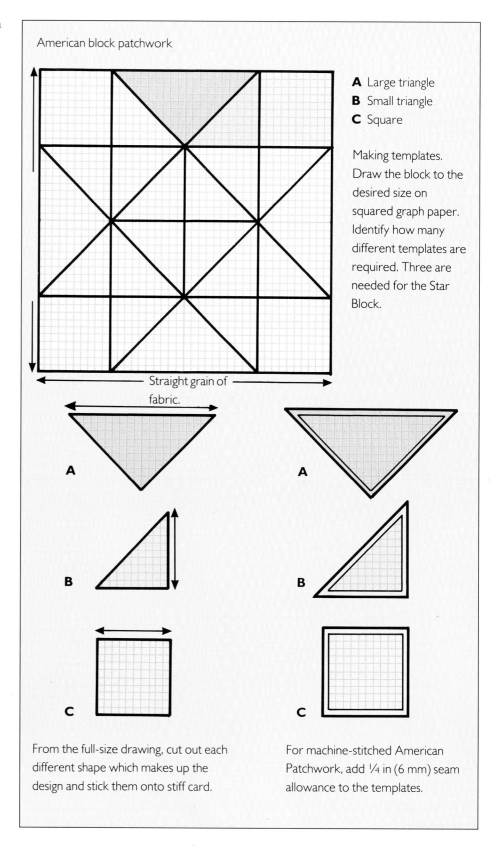

American block patchwork

A Large triangle
B Small triangle
C Square

Making templates. Draw the block to the desired size on squared graph paper. Identify how many different templates are required. Three are needed for the Star Block.

Straight grain of fabric.

A

B

C

From the full-size drawing, cut out each different shape which makes up the design and stick them onto stiff card.

A

B

C

For machine-stitched American Patchwork, add ¼ in (6 mm) seam allowance to the templates.

STITCHING THE BLOCKS TOGETHER

The stitch used to assemble the block is a small, straight running-stitch, hand or machine sewn.

HAND-STITCHED BLOCKS

The line you have marked around each template is the stitching line. Place patches right sides together and pin, with the marked stitching lines matching up.

Stitching should start and end at each seam line (not the edge of the fabric: see diagrams). Begin with a small knot or back-stitch and finish firmly with a back-stitch to prevent the seam coming undone. Press the seam allowances to one side, best, where possible, to do this to the darker fabric side.

Hand-stitched American Patchwork.

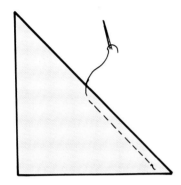

a

Start and end the seam on the marked stitching line.

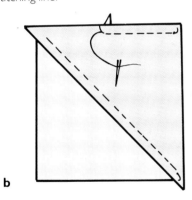

b

Press seams to one side, the darker side if possible.

MACHINE-STITCHED BLOCKS

Place patches right sides together, pin, then guide the raw edges of the fabric against the presser foot of the machine. The foot on most sewing machines will automatically give ¼ in (6 mm) seam allowance. If yours does not, use a narrow strip of masking tape to mark the plate on your machine, parallel to the seam line and ¼ in (6 mm) from the needle. Machine-stitched seams are stronger and can be pressed open (see diagrams).

PIECING ANGLED SHAPES

When joining shapes that meet at an angle other than a right angle, eg. diamonds and triangles, align the stitching lines *not* the cut edges (see diagrams). This makes a straight edge when the patches are opened.

Joining triangles.

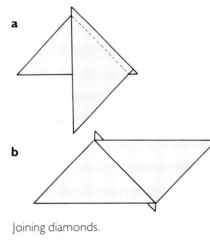

a

b

Joining diamonds.

a

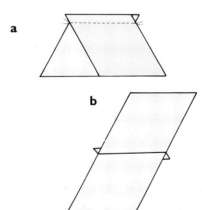

b

Making a rectangle from three triangles.

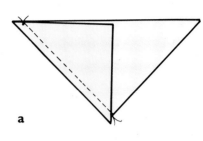

a

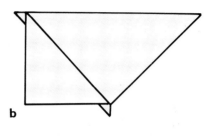

b

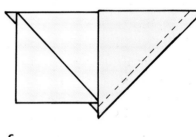

c

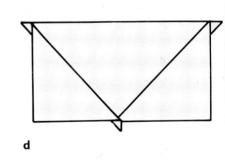

d

Machine-stitched American Patchwork.

a

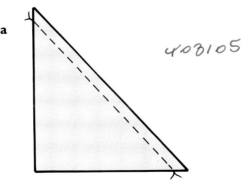

Stitch the seam to the ends of the patches and press it open.

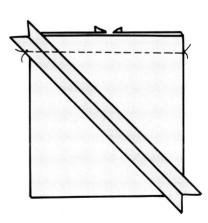

Join to the next patch, again sewing to the edges of the fabric.

A SELECTION OF AMERICAN BLOCKS

Flock

Churn Dash

Railfence

Double Pinwheel

Roman Stripe

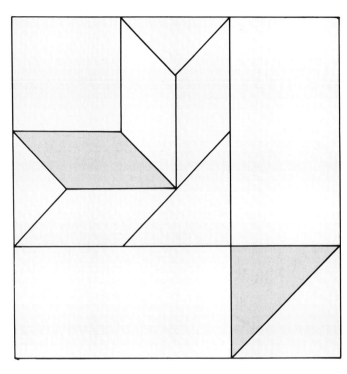

Basket of Scraps

Railroad

Fruit Basket

Dutchman's Puzzle

MATCHING POINTS

Some blocks have a point at which four or more fabrics meet. To match these points accurately, push a pin through at the exact spot where the points are to be matched, at a right angle to your stitching line (see diagram). Stitch up to the pin, remove carefully and stitch over the point.

Pinned and ready to stitch.

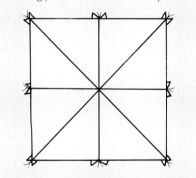

Matching points on seams exactly.

ORDER OF PIECING

The simple Star Block is used to demonstrate the piecing order and construction of an American Block.

TEMPLATES

Three are required: large triangle A, small triangle B, square C.

Following the instruction on p 10, draw the block and make templates as described for hand or machine stitching.

FABRICS REQUIRED

Small pieces of fabric in light, medium and dark values. These can be plain, patterned or a combination of both.

CUTTING OUT

In light fabric cut four A and four C. In dark fabric cut twelve B. In medium fabric cut four B.

Piecing order for Star Block.

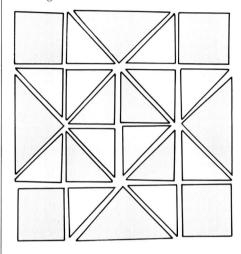

Arrange patches in correct position.

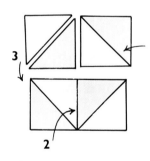

Make up the centre.

Top left – 2 separate triangles.
Top right – 2 triangles formed to join a square.
Bottom – 2 squares joined to form a rectangle.
Final seam joining rectangles into a square indicated by arrow no. 3.

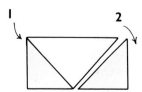

Making the star points (see diagrams for piecing angled shapes).

Join centre to top and bottom star points.

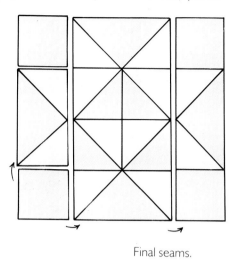

Final seams.

Join side star points to corner squares.

MAKING UP

Arrange the patches on a flat surface in the correct design. Starting with the smaller shapes, piece the block together into larger units (see diagrams). Join into strips wherever possible so you can sew in long straight lines. Press seams as you progress.

APPLIQUÉ

The term appliqué derives from the French word meaning "to apply" and is the technique in which pieces of material are cut and stitched to a background fabric. Appliqué is in many ways a very flexible technique, lending itself to representational design and pictorial motifs such as flower wreaths, animals and birds. These can be seen in many of the old quilts still in existence. The two techniques of patchwork and appliqué are often successfully combined, notably in the block quilts which use a repeated unit of design. Appliqué can also be used to create one large picture over the surface of an entire quilt, a well-known example of this is the "Tree of Life" design.

Appliqué can be done either by hand or machine with the raw edges turned under, or if you are sewing with a swing-needle machine, a close satin-stitch can be used

ABOVE 19th-century Garden Wreath quilt. The quilt is divided into a number of blocks and shows appliquéd spray and wreath patterns combined with patchwork maple leaves. (The American Museum in Britain.)

APPLIQUÉ

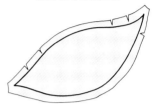

Draw round the template on the wrong side of the fabric.

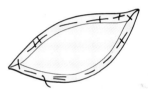

Cut out, allowing ¼ in (6 mm) seam turning; clip inward curves.

Turn the raw edges in and tack down the turning.

Pin and tack, then stitch down.

Machine appliqué using satin stitch.

to cover the raw edges and stitch down the pieces simultaneously.

Templates can be drawn freehand, traced from patterns or made from folded and cut paper. They are made the actual size the piece is to be and seam allowance, if required, is added as you cut the fabric. Place the template face down on the back of the fabric, draw round it with a fabric marker and cut out, adding the desired seam allowance. If you plan to turn under the raw edges, clip any inward curves up to the marked line, turn under the edges and press. Now position the piece on the background, pin and baste in position then hem down with neat stitches, using a thread that matches the piece (see diagram). Where several pieces are used, in a picture for example, the edge of one piece may overlap another. In this case it is not necessary to turn under the raw edges of the piece to be overlapped. When the pieces have been stitched down to the background, to reduce its thickness and make quilting easier, cut away the background fabric behind the appliquéd piece ¼ in (6 mm) in from the sewing line with a pair of sharp scissors.

QUILTING

The quilting stitch is basically a small running-stitch, both functional and decorative, which holds the three layers – the top, filler and backing – of the quilted items together. Whatever the size of your chosen project, the three layers must be thoroughly basted together before quilting begins so that there is no shifting of the layers which may form tucks or pleats on the back or front. Smooth out the backing fabric and the batting together on a flat surface and lay the patchwork on top. Leave a margin of 1–2 in (2.5–5 cm) of backing and batting all round the outer edges. Pin the three layers together, smoothing out the folds from the centre and baste in a grid about 4 in (10.2 cm) apart. Finally baste all round the outer edges.

QUILTING PATTERNS

Contour quilting echoes the shape of the patches, outlining them with a row of stitching ⅜ in (1 cm) from the seams.

Stencils are available for more elaborate quilting designs and include motifs such as cables, feathers, flowers and shells, as well as geometric background patterns (see diagrams). A close web of

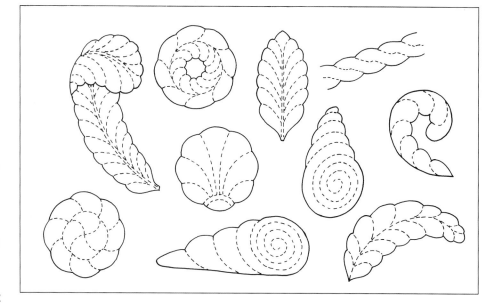

Traditional quilting designs.

quilting was necessary on old quilts to keep the raw wool or cotton filler in place but less stitching is needed for the modern bonded battings. Nevertheless, close quilting is still admired today for the added texture it gives.

HAND QUILTING

Use a fine needle (no. 8, 9, or 10 in "Betweens") and cotton thread about 16 in (40 cm) long. Thread for hand quilting is slightly thicker than machine thread. To avoid knots, pull the thread through beeswax and, working with a single strand, knot the end and come up from the back, tugging the thread to pull the knot through into the batting. Taking small running-stitches and keeping them

as even as possible, make sure each one goes through all three layers.

Small projects can be quilted on the lap but for larger quilts a hoop or frame makes the job easier, holding the fabric as you work. When the thread is finished, tie a knot close to the surface and pull through between the layers, then clip the thread.

MACHINE QUILTING

Preparation must be as thorough for machine quilting as for hand quilting. Small projects can be quickly quilted by machine after basting. Contour quilting around each shape is easy: just use the width of the presser foot to measure an equal distance from the seams. Alternatively, you can machine quilt in the "ditch" of the seams, burying the stitching so it becomes invisible. A walking foot will facilitate machine quilting: this feeds all layers of fabric evenly through the machine. For larger machine-quilted items, the same rules apply: thorough preparation to prevent tucks appearing on the back as you quilt.

For a very large quilt, I recommend quilting in two pieces then joining. Use threads that match the fabrics as far possible or try the invisible thread which has been developed for machine quilting.

To start and finish, do several back-stitches and cut the thread close to the surface.

Cathedral Window
Pincushion

FINISHING TOUCHES

Quilts and smaller projects often need to be bound to neaten the edges. This can be done with straight or bias binding.

STRAIGHT BINDING

A double binding is easier to handle and gives a neater and stronger finish. Cut the binding across the straight grain of the fabric to the length required and between 2–2½ in (5.1–6.4 cm) in width, depending on the project. Fold in half lengthwise and press, with any seams inside. Now baste the binding onto the right side with all raw edges together and stitch through all thicknesses, taking ¼ in (6 mm) seam allowance. The folded edge can now be turned over to enclose the raw edges and hemmed neatly down. At the corners, neaten the ends by turning in the raw edges or mitre, following the diagrams (right).

Mitring Straight Binding

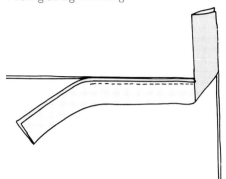

Pin binding to the front of the quilt, raw edges together. At the corner, fold the binding up at a 90° angle and press a crease.

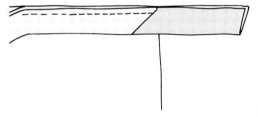

Stitch up to the crease through all thicknesses.

Turn the corner, folding the binding up against the previous crease, and stitch down the second edge.

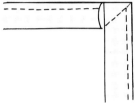

When binding is attached all round the edge of the quilt, join the two ends, pressing the seam open then folding the binding in half to make a continuous strip. Complete the line of stitching over the join.

back

Fold the binding over to the back and hem down. Fold mitre down at corners as you stitch.

Cut strips diagonally across a square of fabric.

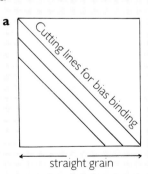

straight grain

To join, place straight-grain edges together.

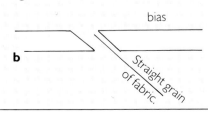

bias

b

Straight grain of fabric.

Stitch right sides together taking ¼ in (6 mm) seam allowance, then press seams! open.

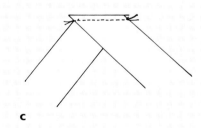

c

Fold in half lengthwise and press again.

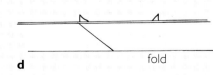

d

fold

BIAS BINDING

Bias binding is stretchy and therefore useful on items with curved edges. To make bias binding, measure the required length and cut across the diagonal of a square of fabric in 2–2½ in (5.1–6.4 cm) widths. Join where necessary, seaming on the straight grain (see diagrams). Press these seams open then fold in half lengthwise and press again. Trim off seam extensions. Bias binding can be stretched and fitted round curves and corners.

OVEN GLOVES

The finished size is 31 in × 7 in

(78.7 cm × 17.8 cm).

MATERIALS REQUIRED

Based on 44 in (112 cm) fabric.
► Plain fabric: ½ yd (½ metre)
► Patterned fabric: ¼ yd (¼ metre)
► Lining: ¼ yd (¼ metre)
► 2–oz batting ¼ yd (¼ metre)

THE PATCHWORK

All measurements include a ¼ in (6 mm) seam allowance.

From the plain fabric cut 23 strips 7½ in × 1¼ in (19.1 cm × 3.2 cm). From the patterned fabric cut 24 strips 7½ in × 1¾ in (19.1 cm × 4.4 cm). Stitch the strips together, alternately plain and patterned, taking ¼ in (6 mm) seam allowance (see diagram 1). Press seams.

MAKING THE GLOVES

Cut a piece of lining and a piece of batting slightly larger all round than the patchwork. Sandwich the batting between the lining and patchwork. Before pinning the three layers, cut two additional squares of batting 7½ in (19.1 cm) and place these 7 in (17.8 cm) in from each end of the rectangle to provide extra insulation for the hands. Smooth the layers together, pin and baste (see diagram 2).

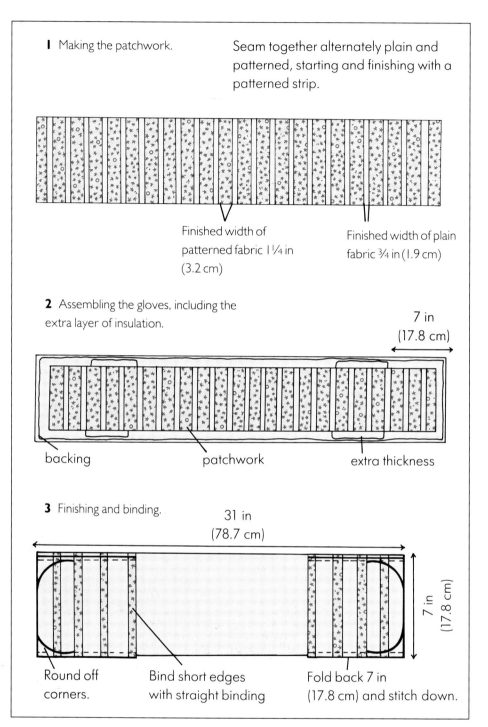

1 Making the patchwork. Seam together alternately plain and patterned, starting and finishing with a patterned strip.

Finished width of patterned fabric 1¼ in (3.2 cm)

Finished width of plain fabric ¾ in (1.9 cm)

2 Assembling the gloves, including the extra layer of insulation.

7 in (17.8 cm)

backing   patchwork   extra thickness

3 Finishing and binding.

31 in (78.7 cm)

7 in (17.8 cm)

Round off corners.

Bind short edges with straight binding

Fold back 7 in (17.8 cm) and stitch down.

QUILTING AND FINISHING

Quilt close to the seams on the patterned strips. Trim the width down to 7 in (17.8 cm). Bind the short ends with plain fabric to neaten. Fold back the ends to form pockets 7 in (17.8 cm) deep and stitch down the sides (see diagram 3). Trim the corners, rounding them off through all thicknesses.

Measure all round the outside of the oven gloves and cut enough bias binding from the plain fabric 2½ in (5.7 cm) wide, joining where necessary. Fold, wrong sides together, and press.

Stitch binding all round the outside, turn over and stitch down to neaten the raw edges. Finish with a hanging loop in plain fabric.

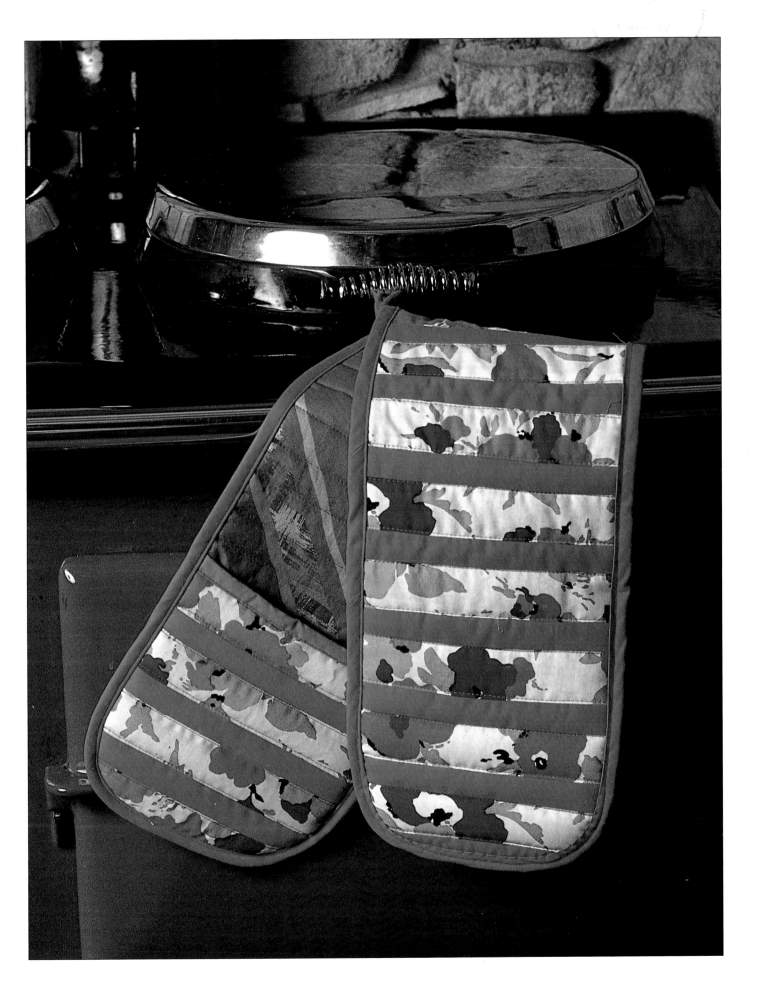

OVEN MITT

. . . .

This is a quick and easy project which needs a sewing machine and optional rotary cutter. The finished size is approx 11 in × 8 in (30 cm × 22 cm).

MATERIALS REQUIRED

▶ 4–oz batting: 20 in × 13 in (50.8 cm × 33 cm)
▶ Plain fabric: ½ yd (½ metre)
▶ Patterned fabric: 1 yd (1 metre)

MAKING THE MITT

From the plain fabric cut 12 strips, each 10 in × 1¼ in (25.4 cm × 3.2 cm).

From the patterned fabric cut 12 strips, each 10 in × 1¾ in (25.4 cm × 4.4 cm).

Cut the batting into two pieces, each 10 in × 13 in (25.4 cm × 33.0 cm).

The strips of fabric are joined and quilted onto the batting simultaneously in the "Quilt as you go" method, shown in diagram 1.

Place a plain strip of fabric right side up along one narrow edge of batting then pin a patterned strip over this with right sides together and raw edges even. Stitch through the two strips and the batting ¼ in (6 mm) from the raw edges then fold the patterned strip over and flat against the batting. Finger press (do not iron batting).

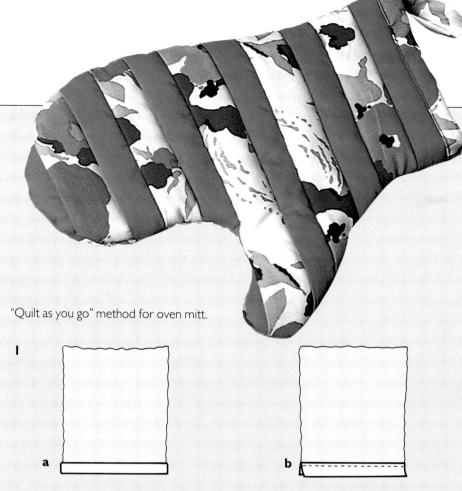

"Quilt as you go" method for oven mitt.

I

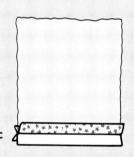

a Place strip 1 along one narrow edge of batting right side up.

b Place strip 2 right side down on top of strip 1 and stitch through all layers.

c Fold over and finger press.

d Continue adding strips until batting is covered.

2

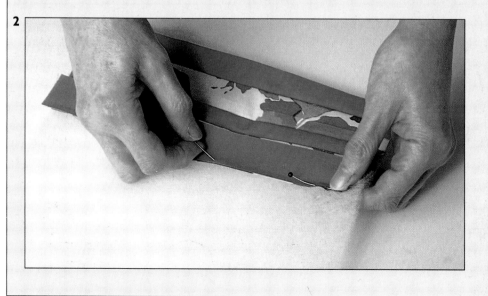

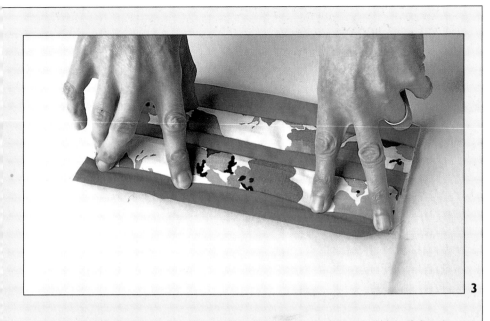

Take a second plain strip and place this face down against the patterned strip and pin down with raw edges even. Stitch through all three layers as before taking ¼ in (6 mm) seam allowance. Fold the plain strip flat against the batting and finger press as before. Continue building alternate plain and patterned strips onto the batting until it is covered. Repeat so you have two pieces of covered batting.

Draught the mitt pattern onto paper using the chart and cut out a paper template (see diagram 4). A seam allowance of ¼ in (6 mm) is included.

Place the paper template onto one of the pieces of patchwork, pin and cut out carefully. Now place this half mitt against the other piece of patchwork, right sides together, and pin. Stitch round the outer edge taking ¼ in (6 mm) seam allowance. Leave the wrist open. Now trim away excess fabric from the second piece of patchwork and clip into the curve between thumb and hand. Turn the mitt inside out, batting inside.

THE LINING

Place the remaining patterned fabric pieces right sides together. Pin the paper mitt template down and cut out, adding an extra 1½ in (3.8 cm) at the wrist. Stitch together on the stitching line taking ⅜ in (1 cm) seam allowance. (This larger allowance will help the lining to fit neatly inside the mitt.) Neaten the raw edges on the wrist by folding ½ in (1.3 cm) in then push the lining inside the mitt. Fold the extra lining fabric over the wrist and stitch through all layers on the outside.

FINISHING

Make a loop of patterned fabric and stitch to the inside of the mitt for hanging.

Pattern for oven mitt.   Each square represents 1½ in (3.8 cm).

clip into curve when stitched

¼ in (6mm) seam allowance included

For the lining, add an extra 1½ in (3.8 cm) here.

12 in (30.5 cm)

9 in (22.9 cm)

TABLECLOTH

This unusual hexagonal-shaped tablecloth requires only one template. Use all your delicate floral prints for a touch of nostalgia. The finished size is 47 in × 41 in (119.4 cm × 104.1 cm).

MATERIALS REQUIRED
▶ A variety of small pieces of fabric in medium- and light-value floral prints
▶ Muslin (calico) for the edging diamonds: ¾ yd (¾ metre)
▶ Backing fabric: 47 in × 41 in (119.m × 104.1 cm)
▶ Floral fabric for binding: ½ yd (½ metre)

MAKING THE STAR POINTS
Trace the template (see diagram 1). Seam allowance is not included so either add this to the template or when cutting out the fabrics. For each point of the centre star you will need 25 diamonds. Arrange them on a flat surface alternately in a medium/light sequence. Stitch together in rows of five, then stitch the rows together (see picture 2). (See Seaming Angled Shapes and Matching Points in Chapter 1, pp 11–12.) Press seams open or to one side. Make six star points.

JOINING THE STAR POINTS
Join the star points in two sets of three, then put the two halves together and stitch the final seam across the centre of

the star (see diagram 3). Leave ¼ in (6 mm) unstitched at each inner angle.

THE OUTER DIAMONDS
For each of the six outer diamonds, using the template cut five from patterned fabric and 20 from plain. Join as for the star points, placing the patterned shapes down the centre of each large diamond. Position the outer diamonds between the star points, pin and stitch, right sides together (see diagrams).

At the inner angle of the points turn the outer diamond through the unstitched seam allowance.

Press seams towards the star. Stay stitch the outer edge within the seam allowance.

THE BACKING
Smooth the backing fabric and the patchwork together, wrong sides facing. Trim the backing to fit leaving an extra 1 in (2.5 cm) all round the outside. Pin and baste the two layers together. Hand or machine quilt to secure the backing and patchwork together.

THE BINDING
Cut bias strips 2 in (5.1 cm) wide and long enough to go round the outside of the tablecloth, seaming where necessary. Fold the binding in half lengthwise (wrong sides together), baste and stitch to the right side of the cloth, all raw edges together. Turn to the back and hand hem over the raw edges.

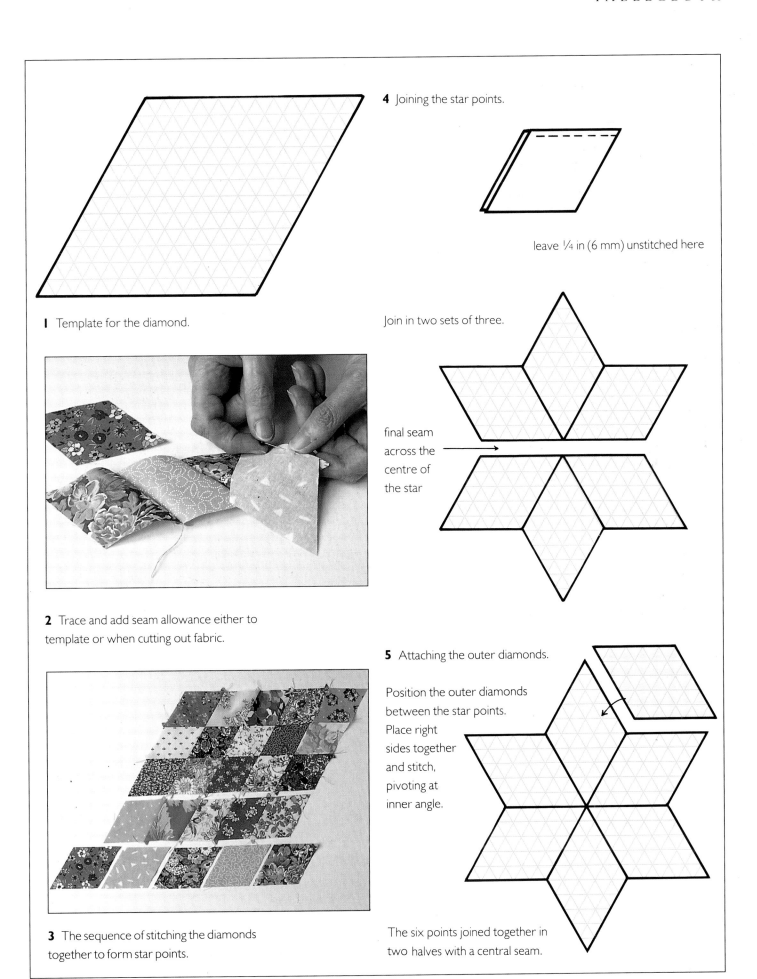

1 Template for the diamond.

2 Trace and add seam allowance either to template or when cutting out fabric.

3 The sequence of stitching the diamonds together to form star points.

4 Joining the star points.

leave ¼ in (6 mm) unstitched here

Join in two sets of three.

final seam across the centre of the star

5 Attaching the outer diamonds.

Position the outer diamonds between the star points. Place right sides together and stitch, pivoting at inner angle.

The six points joined together in two halves with a central seam.

STAR PILLOW

The finished size is 18 in × 18 in

(46 cm × 46 cm).

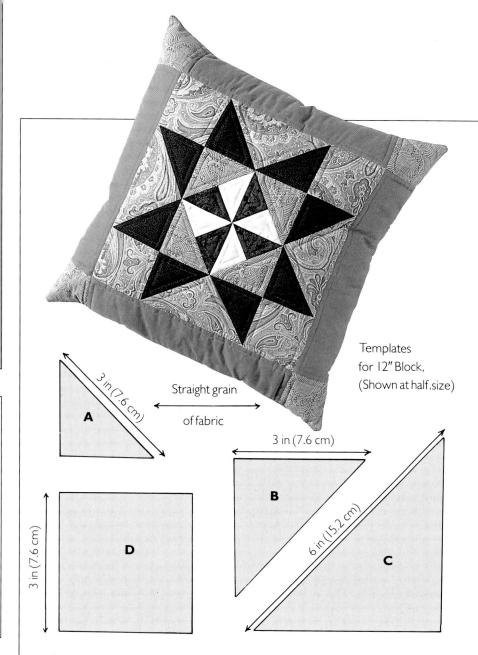

MATERIALS REQUIRED

Based on 44 in (132 cm) wide fabric.

▶ Block: small pieces in two dark-value fabrics, one medium-value and two light-value

▶ Plain fabric for the borders and back: ½ yd (½ metre)

▶ Light-coloured sheeting or similar for the lining: ½ yd (½ metre)

▶ 2–oz batting: 20 in (50 cm) square

▶ 16–in (40–cm) zipper

MAKING THE BLOCK CENTRE

Draw the block full-size (see diagram 1) and make templates as described in Chapter 1. Make one small triangle A, one medium triangle B, one large triangle C and one square D. Cut out patches in these colour values:

A: four light; four dark

B: four medium; eight dark

C: four light

D: four light

Borders: four strips plain 12½ in (31.6 cm) × 3½ in (8.8 cm)

Corners: four medium-value, 3½ in (8.8 cm) squares

N.B. Measurements for the border strips and squares include a ¼ in (6 mm) seam allowance.

Make the centre with four dark-value and four light-value A triangles plus four

I The block and the templates.

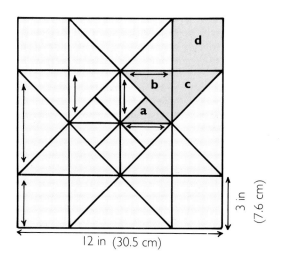

Draw the block full-size and make templates. Add ¼ in (6 mm) seam allowance either to the templates or when cutting out the fabric pieces.

Templates for 12″ Block, (Shown at half size)

Straight grain of fabric

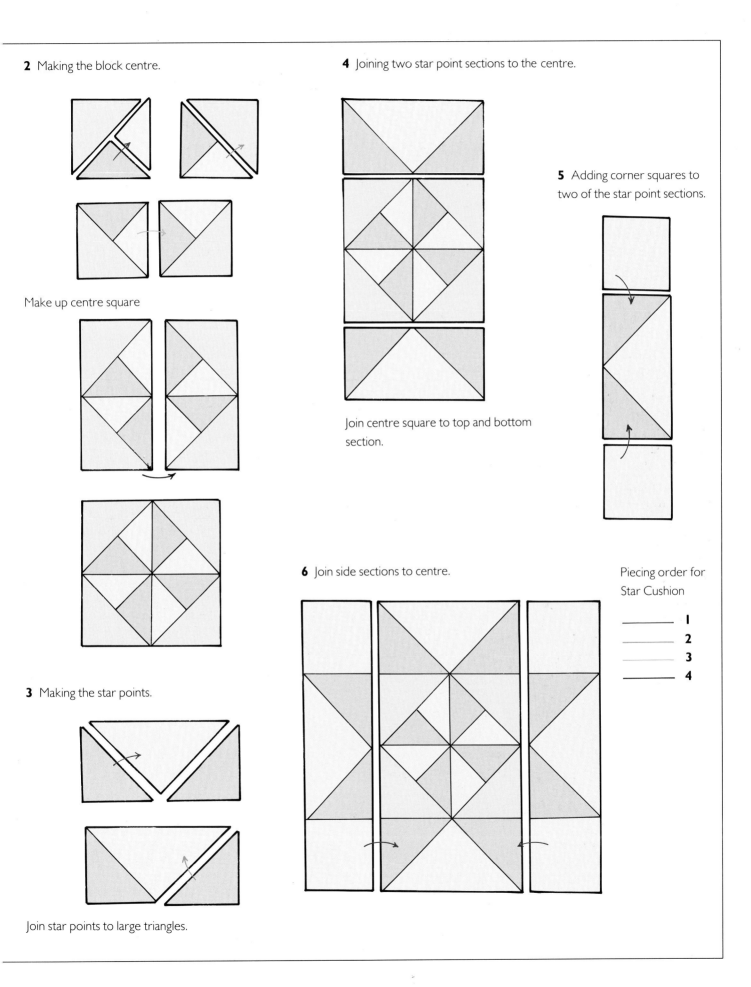

2 Making the block centre.

Make up centre square

3 Making the star points.

Join star points to large triangles.

4 Joining two star point sections to the centre.

Join centre square to top and bottom section.

5 Adding corner squares to two of the star point sections.

6 Join side sections to centre.

Piecing order for Star Cushion

——————— 1
——————— 2
——————— 3
——————— 4

7 The completed block with borders and squares.

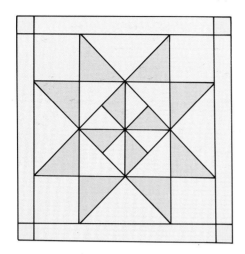

8 Insert the zipper in the seam.

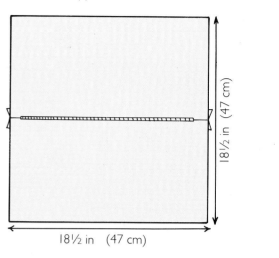

18½ in (47 cm)

18½ in (47 cm)

medium-value B triangles (see diagram 2). Make the star points with four light-value C triangles and eight dark-value B triangles (see diagram 3). Join two star point sections to the centre square (see diagram 4). Join corner D squares to the other two star point sections (see diagram 5) and join these side sections to the centre (see diagram 6).

THE BORDERS AND CORNERS

For the border and corner squares, stitch two of the border strips to opposite sides of the block. Add corner squares to each end of the other two border strips and stitch these along the remaining edges of the block (see diagram 7). Press the block with a steam or dry iron and damp cloth.

QUILTING THE BLOCK

Measure the block and cut pieces of batting and lining slightly larger all around (about 1 in/2.5 cm). Sandwich the batting between the patchwork and lining, with right sides of the fabrics outwards. Pin the three layers together, making sure there are no tucks or wrinkles on the back or front. Baste the three layers together in a grid with stitches approximately 3 in (7.5 cm) apart, then baste around the edge. Quilt ¼ in (6 mm) in from each seam by hand or machine.

FINISHING

Cut two pieces of backing fabric (the same fabric as the border strips) half the size of the patchwork top plus ½ in (1.25 cm) extra on one side. Join the seam, leaving a gap for the zipper. Press the seam open, then insert the zipper (see diagram 8).

Place the patchwork front and cushion back right sides together with zipper closed. Stitch together through all layers taking ¼ in (6 mm) seam allowance. Trim the seam and finish with a zigzag stitch. Open the zipper and turn right sides out.

FOLDED LOG CABIN PILLOW

. . . .

This is a Log Cabin block with a difference: instead of the strips lying flat against the backing fabric they are cut and folded, then overlapped revealing ½ in (1.3 cm) of fabric. The folds lift away from the backing, giving an interesting surface texture to the block. The finished size is 15 in × 15 in (38.1 cm × 38.1 cm).

MATERIALS REQUIRED

Based on 44 in (112 cm) wide fabric.
► Lightweight cotton backing, eg, sheeting in a pale colour: four pieces each 10 in (25.4 cm) square
► Block centres: a small piece of fabric in a strong colour, 4 in × 16 in (10.2 cm × 40.6 cm)
► Strips: four dark- and four light-toned fabrics: ¼ yd (¼ metre) of each
► Fabric for the frame and back of the pillow: ½ yd (½ metre)

1 Centre template for folded Log Cabin block.

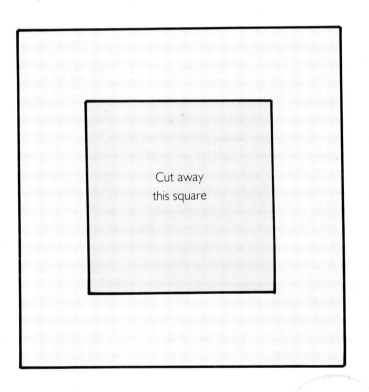

Cut away this square

2 Block centre in position on backing.

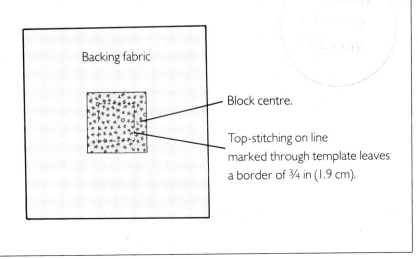

Backing fabric

Block centre.

Top-stitching on line marked through template leaves a border of ¾ in (1.9 cm).

27

THE BLOCK CENTRE

Make up four blocks together.

Make a template for the block centre by tracing diagram 1 onto card and cutting out the shaded area. Cut the block centres 3½ in (8.9 cm) square. Place and pin these centrally on top of each backing square. Position the template over these and mark a 2 in (5.1 cm) square through the window. Top stitch on the line with straight- or satin-stitch. This leaves a border of ¾ in (1.9 cm) round the edges (see diagram 2).

FIRST ROUND OF STRIPS

Take the first light fabric and from the full width cut strips 2½ in (6.4 cm) wide. Fold in half lengthwise (wrong sides together) and press. This makes the strip 1¼ in (3.2 cm) wide when folded. Mark the stitching line ½ in (1.3 cm) from the folded edge on all strips. Place strip 1 against the top-stitching on the block centre, cut length fo fit (3½ in/8.9 cm) and stitch down ½ in (1.3 cm) from the fold on the marked line. Turn the block one quarter turn, place strip 2 against the top-stitching as before and cut to fit (4 in/10.2 cm). Stitch down ½ in (1.3 cm) from the fold through all thicknesses.

Take the first dark fabric, cut strips 2½ in (6.4 cm) wide, press in half and mark the stitching line ½ in (1.3 cm) from the fold as before. Turn the block a quarter turn and place strip 3 against the top-stitching on the third side of the block centre. Cut to fit (4 in/10.2 cm) and stitch down as before. Turn the block a quarter turn again and add strip 4. This completes the first round (see diagram 3).

SECOND ROUND OF STRIPS

Take the second light fabric, cut strips, press the fold and mark the stitching line as for the first round. Place the fold against the previous line of stitching (on round one). Cut the strip to fit (4½ in/11.4 cm) and stitch down. Repeat for strip 6 in light fabric and strips 7 and 8 in dark fabric (see diagram 4).

3 The first round of strips.

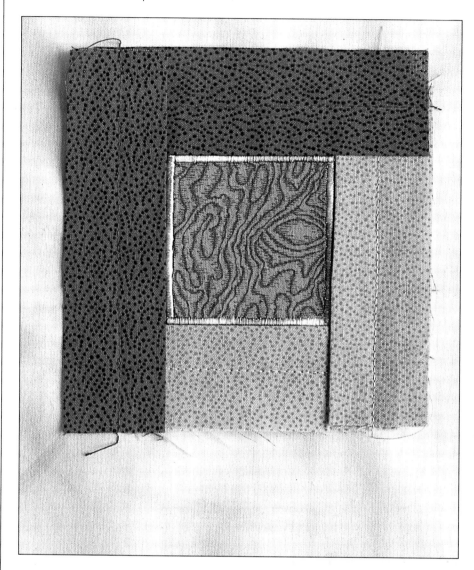

4 The second round of strips.

5 The third round of strips.

6 The fourth round of strips.

7 The frame around the block.

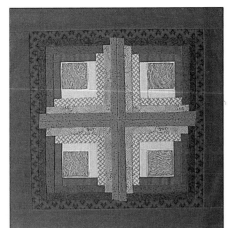

THIRD ROUND OF STRIPS

The extra seam allowance of ¾ in (1.9 cm) is not required on the third round as the fourth round is stitched flat against the backing to reduce bulk when joining blocks. Cut all strips for the third round 1½ in (3.8 cm) wide and 5¾ in (14.6 cm) long, fold and press. Mark the stitching line ½ in (1.3 cm) from the fold and stitch down, keeping dark and light fabric in correct sequence (see diagram 5).

FOURTH ROUND OF STRIPS

Cut the strips for round four 1¼ in (3.2 cm) wide. Do not fold these. Place strip 13 (the fourth light fabric) face down along the raw edges of strip 9 and cut length to fit. Stitch down, taking ¼ in (6 mm) seam allowance. Turn the strip over and press flat down against the backing. Repeat for strips 14, 15 and 16, cutting lengths to fit. Press the blocks (see diagram 6).

JOINING THE BLOCKS

Trim the backing fabric from the light sides of each block and reduce strip widths down to ¾ in (1.9 cm). Place the light corners to the centre. Join, taking ¼ in (6 mm) seam allowance through all thicknesses, then press seams open.

THE BLOCK FRAME

Cut the four strips from the ½ yd (½ metre) of fabric to be used for the block frame and pillow back, each 2½ in × 17 in (6.4 cm × 43 cm). Stitch strips to the top and bottom, then the sides of the block (see diagram 7). Press and trim the block to 16½ in (41.9 cm) square.

Make up the back and finish as for Star Cushion, p 24.

WAVE PILLOW

. . . .

A combination of pintucks and folded strips which lift away from the background give this pillow an extra dimension. The finished size is 18 in × 18 in (45.7 cm × 45.7 cm).

MATERIALS REQUIRED

Based on 44 in (112 cm) wide fabric.

► Backing fabric: a piece of sheeting or cotton 18 in (45.7 cm) square

► For the wave panel: small pieces of contrasting fabrics in two designs

► For the first border: a strip of plain fabric 2 in × 36 in (5.2 cm × 91.4 cm)

► For the folded strips: ¼ yd (¼ metre) of dark and ¼ yd (¼ metre) of light fabrics

► For the outer border and back of the pillow: ½ yd (½ metre)

► 14–in (35.6–cm) zipper

MAKING THE WAVE PANEL

All measurements include a ¼ in (6 mm) seam allowance.

From two contrasting fabrics cut ten lighter strips 1⅛ in × 8 in (2.8 cm × 20.3 cm) and nine darker strips 1 in × 8 in (2.5 cm × 20.3 cm). Fold the darker strips in half lengthwise (wrong sides together) and press. Place a folded dark

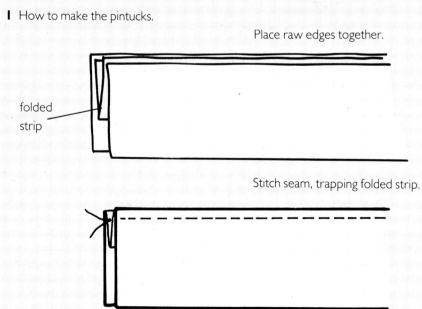

I How to make the pintucks.

Place raw edges together.

folded strip

Stitch seam, trapping folded strip.

2 The stitching line and the tucks pressed upwards.

The centre panel.   Stitching the tucks down the centre.

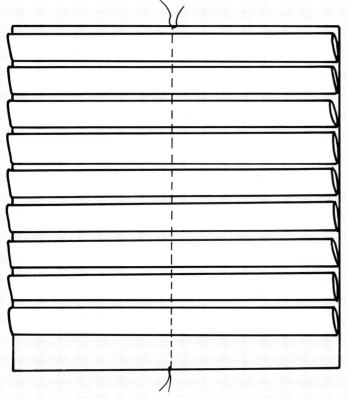

3 Two more stitching lines and the tucks pressed downwards.

For the wave panel, dark and light can be reversed as in this sample.

strip against the right side of one of the light ones, raw edges together and pin another light strip on top. Stitch the two light strips together, trapping the folded strip in the seam and taking scant ¼ in (6 mm) seam allowance (see diagram).

Continue adding the light strips and trapping the folded dark strips in the seams until you have stitched together all the strips. On the back, press all the seams one way, and on the front press all the tucks one way. Trim the panel to 7½ in (19 cm) at the sides.

Draw a vertical line down the centre of the panel and stitch the tucks down against the light strips. Then press the tucks the other way, ie, upwards, on both sides of the line (see diagram 2). Draw two more lines half-way between the centre line and the edges of the panel, and stitch again, fastening the tucks down the other way. Now press the tucks back in the opposite direction either side of these two lines of stitching and fasten them down close to the edges (see diagram 3).

THE FIRST BORDER
Place the wave panel in the centre of the 18 in (45.7 cm) backing square and pin. Using the third fabric cut two strips 2 in × 7½ in (5.1 cm × 19.1 cm). Place these right side down against the top and bottom of the panel, raw edges together and stitch through all layers taking ¼ in (6 mm) seam allowance. Turn these strips over and press flat against the backing. Now cut two more strips in the same fabric 2 in × 10½ in (5.1 cm × 26.7 cm) and repeat at each side of the panel (see diagram 4). Draw a line 1 in (2.5 cm) from the seam and top stitch with straight- or satin-stitch.

THE FOLDED STRIPS

For the first round, take the fourth fabric and cut a strip 2½ in × 44 in (6.4 cm × 112 cm). Fold in half lengthwise (wrong sides together) and press. Mark a stitching line ½ in (1.3 cm) from the folded edge. Place this folded edge against the top stitching on the panel, cut to length and stitch the strips across the top and bottom then across each side, sewing on the marked line (see diagram 5).

The second round of folded strips is in the third fabric. Cut a strip 2½ in (6.4 cm) wide across the width of the fabric. Fold and press, then mark the stitching line ½ in (1.3 cm) from the folded edge as before. Place the fold against the previous line of stitching, cut the length of the strip to fit and stitch to the top, bottom and sides along the marked line.

The third and last round does not need the extra seam allowance because the final border lies flat against the backing. From the fourth fabric cut the strips 1½ in (3.8 cm) wide, fold in half and press, then stitch down ½ in (1.3 cm) from the fold, leaving ¼ in (6 mm) between the stitching line and raw edges.

THE OUTER BORDER

From the ½ yd (½ metre) piece of fabric cut a 3 in (7.6 cm) border. This is to be added all around the outside. Place the border fabric right sides down, first against the top and bottom, then stitch and press the strips flat against the backing. Stitch borders to the sides, again pressing the strips flat down against the backing. Trim the block to 16½ in (41.9 cm). Using the remaining fabric from the ½ yd (½ metre) piece, make up the pillow back, insert the zipper and finish as for the Star Cushion, p 24.

4 Pintuck panel with the first border.

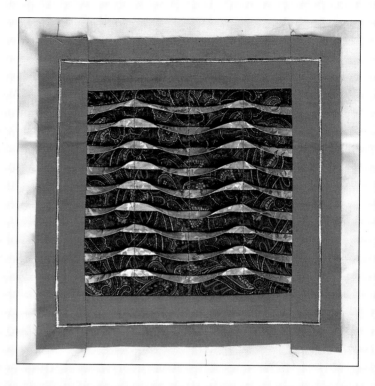

5 The first round of the folded strips.

Adding the folded strips.

Sew a folded strip across the top and bottom, then across each side.

Place folded strip against the line of stitching on inner border and sew down ½ in (1.3 cm) from folded edge.

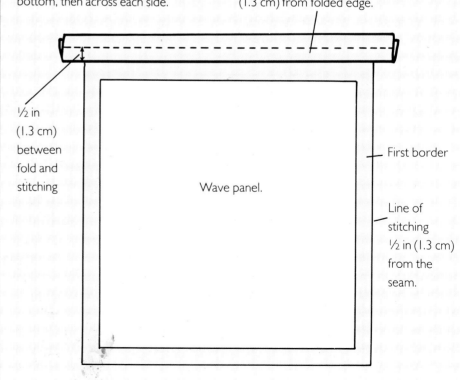

½ in (1.3 cm) between fold and stitching

Wave panel.

First border

Line of stitching ½ in (1.3 cm) from the seam.

HEXAGONAL MOSAIC PILLOW

. . . .

Mosaic or "English" patchwork is another method of sewing the pieces together. Each fabric patch is shaped by basting it onto a paper template which is later removed. Although more time-consuming than American patchwork, it does have the advantage of being able to fit intricate interlocking shapes together. This pillow design uses three shapes: a hexagon, a diamond and a triangle. The finished panel is hexagonal, size 11 in (27.9 cm).

MAKING THE TEMPLATES

Trace the templates (see diagram 1) and cut the three shapes out of the stiff card. Now draw round the card templates onto the paper and cut one hexagon, 18 triangles and 30 diamonds. Alternatively, you can cut the papers directly from isometric graph paper, being careful to cut the shapes the same sizes.

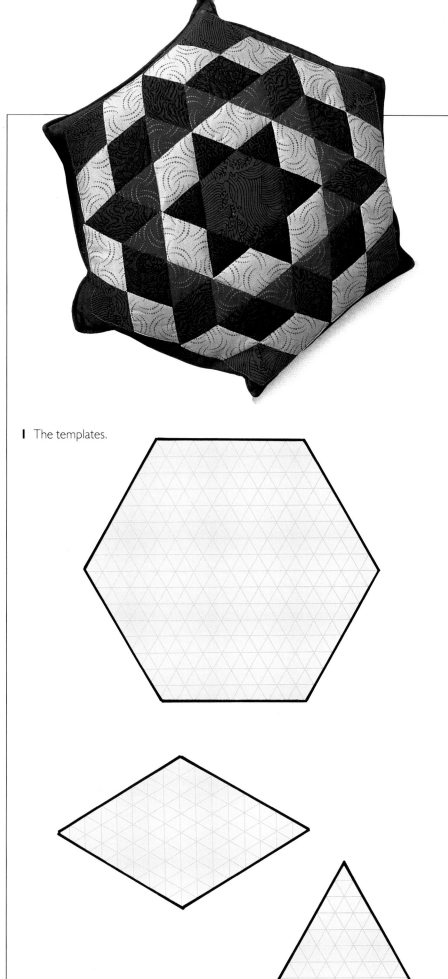

I The templates.

2 Covering the papers.

a Pin paper shape to the wrong side of the fabric and cut out the patch ¼ in–⅜ in (6 mm–9 mm) bigger than the paper all round.

a

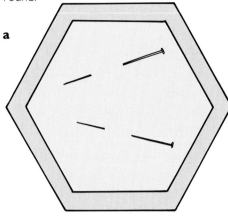

b Fold the fabric over the paper, ensuring that the edge of the paper is right into the fold, and baste through all layers. At the corners fold the fabric over and secure with a stitch.

b

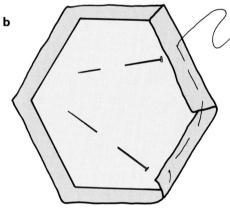

c Finish with one or two back-stitches. Press the patch to form a sharp crease round the edge.

c

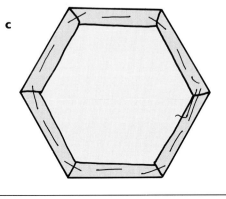

d,e Where the shape has an acute angle, trim the sharp corner off the fabric to reduce bulk.

d

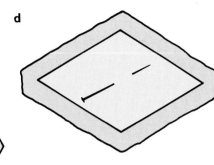

e

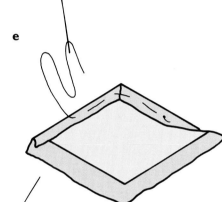

f,g A tab of fabric will project beyond the sharp points. This must be manoeuvred to the back when stitching the patches together.

f

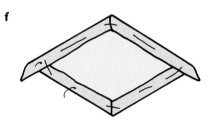

g

MATERIALS REQUIRED

► Plain colour for the back and borders: ½ yd (½ metre)
► Small pieces of fabric in five patterns, three dark-, one medium- and one light-colour value
► Lining: ½ yd (½ metre)
► 2-oz batting: ½ yd (½ metre)
► A hexagonal pillow pad with 7½ in (17.8 cm) sides
► 10 in (25 cm) zipper
► Stiff card: 1 sheet A4
► Good-quality paper or isometric graph paper: five sheets A4

CUTTING THE PATCHES AND COVERING THE PAPERS

Pin the papers to the wrong side of the fabric and cut out the patch approximately ¼ in (6 mm) larger than the paper, 1 hexagon in medium-colour value, 6 triangles in dark-colour value, 12 triangles in medium-colour value, 18 diamonds in light-colour value, 12 diamonds in dark-colour value, 6 diamonds in medium-colour value, 55 patches altogether, and baste firmly (see diagram 2), starting with a knot and finishing with one or two back-stitches. Use a light-coloured thread which can be easily seen to make later removal easier. Press all patches to form a sharp crease round the outside.

JOINING THE PATCHES

Starting with the centre hexagon and six dark triangles, place the edges to be joined right sides together and whip stitch. Begin with a back-stitch or knot and end with several back-stitches (see diagram 3). Now take six light-value diamonds and add each one in turn to the centre (diagram 4). Refer to diagram 5 and piece together the units each made up of one diamond and two triangles (which make a larger triangle) before adding

35

3 Joining the triangles to the hexagon.

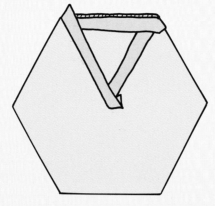

Place patches right sides together and oversew neatly. Try not to catch the paper in the stitching. Begin either with a knot concealed in the seam allowance or 2–3 back-stitches and fasten off firmly with back-stitches.

When the triangles are attached to each side of the centre hexagon, add diamonds.

4 Adding the diamonds.

5 The sequence of completing the block.

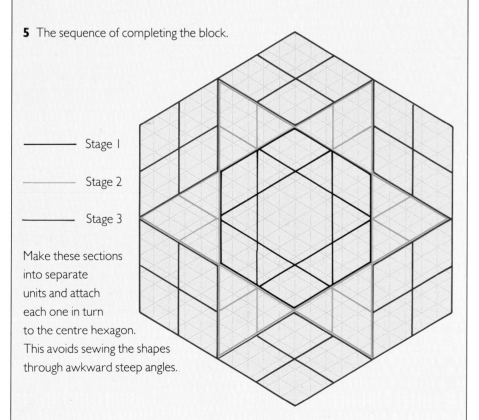

―――― Stage 1

―――― Stage 2

―――― Stage 3

Make these sections into separate units and attach each one in turn to the centre hexagon. This avoids sewing the shapes through awkward steep angles.

them to the centre. Piece together the diamond units (stage 3 diagram 5) before adding them in turn to the centre. This completes the hexagonal-shaped panel. When the panel is complete, press with a steam iron to form a sharp crease round the outside, then carefully remove all the papers.

APPLIQUÉ, QUILTING AND FINISHING

From the ½ yd (½ metre) of fabric allowed for the back of the pillow cut a piece 18 in (45.7 cm) square. Smooth the patchwork onto the centre of this square, pin and baste down. Appliqué the patchwork to the backing by hand or machine. This technique is covered in Chapter 1. Now turn over and trim away the backing fabric under the patchwork ¼ in (6 mm) from the seam to reduce bulk.

Cut pieces of lining and batting to fit the patchwork and pin and baste together. Quilt as preferred. The example shown here was quilted by machine in the ditch of the seams to outline the patches and emphasise the mosaic shapes.

Now measure your hexagonal pillow and adjust the size of the panel to fit, including enough seam allowance for joining to the back of the pillow. Cut out the hexagon shape. From the remaining fabric make up the pillow back and insert the zipper across the centre (see diagram 7), as for Star Cushion, p 24. Leave the back as a rectangle. Pin the hexagonal panel onto the back, right sides together, and stitch. Trim away excess fabric from the back and neaten the edges with a zigzag stitch. Turn right side out and press then top stitch ⅛ in (3 mm) from the outside edges all the way round.

DELECTABLE SCRAPS QUILT

. . . .

A traditional block design

"Delectable Mountains" is used in

this scrap quilt, hence its name.

The finished size is 89 in

(226 cm) square.

MATERIALS REQUIRED

▶ Cotton backing fabric: 6 yd
 (6 metres)

▶ 2–oz batting: 6 yd (6 metres)

▶ Scraps in assorted patterned and
 plain fabrics

Estimating fabrics for this type of scrap quilt is quite difficult, if not impossible, but if you run out of one colour or design you can always substitute another. I can only give the finished size of the quilt and recommend that you begin with a large collection of different cotton dress-weight scraps. Pieces need not necessarily be large, in fact, the small triangles may use leftover bits of fabric too small for other projects.

THE BLOCKS

Make templates for triangles A, B, C and D, as shown in diagram 1.

Join the triangles in the order shown in diagram 2.

I The templates for a block.

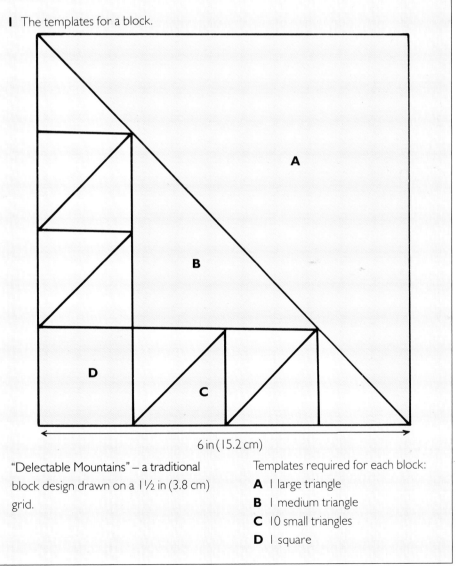

"Delectable Mountains" – a traditional block design drawn on a 1½ in (3.8 cm) grid.

Templates required for each block:

A I large triangle
B I medium triangle
C 10 small triangles
D I square

6 in (15.2 cm)

2 Order of joining the pieces for one block.

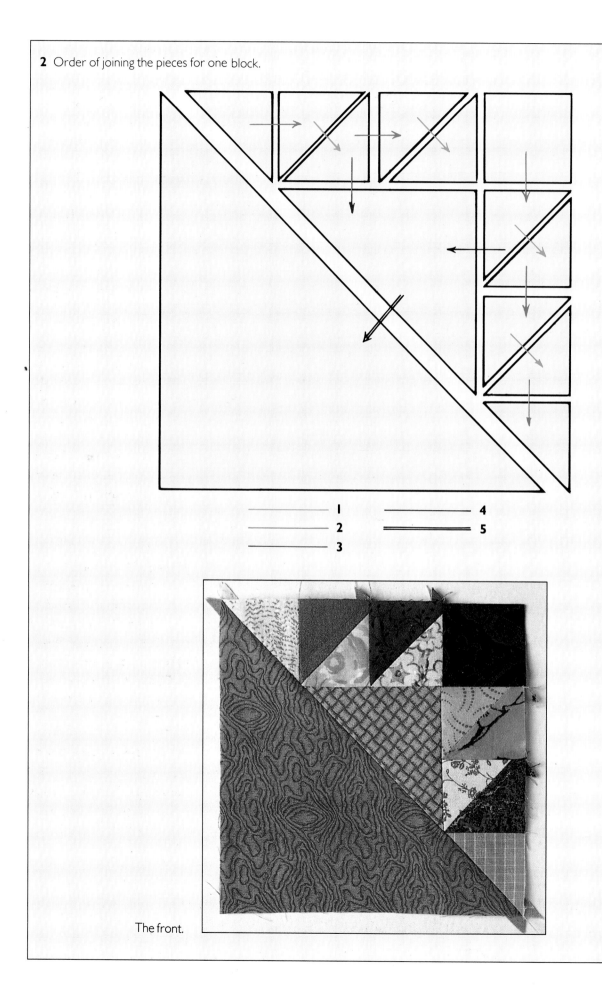

———————— 1	———————— 4
———————— 2	════════ 5
———————— 3	

The front.

As you make up the blocks, follow these simple rules to achieve a similar effect. Plain and patterned fabrics can be mixed. When piecing the individual blocks, aim for a good dark/light contrast between the small triangles so that the "mountain" effect is fairly obvious. In each set of four blocks (diagram 3) I included one large, dark triangle, arranged so that these were spread out evenly over the surface of the quilt. As the blocks are completed you can join them in sets of four as illustrated. The quilt contains 36 sets of four blocks: 144 blocks altogether.

When you have made all the blocks, join them in sets of four (see diagram 3). Arrange the four-block units together on a large, flat surface, making sure none of the same fabrics are placed edge to edge. If you are planning to hand quilt, the top may be made up in one piece. As this quilt was machine quilted, I made the top in two pieces and quilted them first before finally joining them together as described below.

THE BORDER
A 6 in (15.2 cm) wide border of 1 in (2.5 cm) and 1½ in (3.8 cm) randomly pieced strips is separated from the blocks by narrow, plain strips of fabric ¾ in (1.9 cm) wide, each one the length of a four-block panel (see diagram 4). There are plain squares at each corner and the quilt is finished with a navy-blue straight binding.

QUILTING AND FINISHING
If quilting by hand, when the quilt top is completed press on the front and back and assemble with the backing and batting. Baste thoroughly in a 4 in (10.2 cm) grid and then quilt.

If quilting by machine, work each of the two pieces separately but leave a 6 in (15.2 cm) unquilted channel along the edges which are to be joined. In this case the border is attached to one long side and two short sides of each piece and matched

The back.

3 Four blocks joined together.

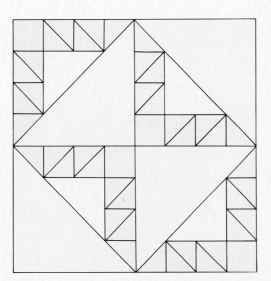

up when the two pieces are joined. To join the two pieces together, place the tops right sides together. Match the triangle points and pin the two top pieces only together, not the batting or backing, and stitch.

Press the seam then lay the quilt face down on a large table and trim the batting edge to edge. Join flat with a herringbone stitch. Lap one side of the backing over the other, trim away excess fabric, turn under a narrow hem and hand stitch the two backing pieces together with a neat hemming-stitch. Machine quilt the channel in the centre of the quilt.

BINDING

Cut lengths of straight binding, 2½ in (6.4 cm) wide, joining as necessary. Fold lengthwise and press. Pin to the quilt edges on the right side, raw edges together. Stitch all round, mitring the corners (see Chapter 1). Turn the binding over to the quilt back and hem down.

4 Detail showing how the border is made, plus the four-block-long strip of plain fabric.

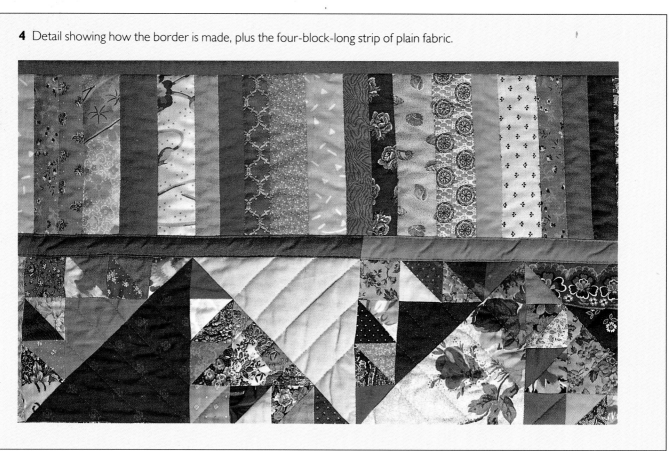

CRIB QUILT AND MATCHING SCALED-DOWN DOLL'S QUILT

· · · · · · · · · · ·

What better way to welcome a new baby than with this simple, traditional crib quilt and, if there is already a little girl in the family, make the scaled-down doll's quilt to include her in the event. The finished sizes are: crib quilt 31 in × 35 in (78.7 cm × 88.9 cm), doll's quilt 20 in × 17 in (50.8 cm × 43.2 cm).

MATERIALS REQUIRED

► Dress-weight cotton in small prints: 56 pieces each 2 ½ in × 10½ in (6.4 cm × 26 cm). These can be all different to give a scrap-quilt look or, if you do not have a collection of many different fabrics, some can be repeated.

► For the border: ½ yd (½ metre) cotton

► Backing: 1 yd (1 metre) cotton

► 2–oz batting: 37 in × 33 in (94 cm × 84 cm)

MAKING THE PATCHWORK

All measurements include ¼ in (6 mm) seam allowance.

Cut 56 strips 2½ in × 10½ in (6.4 cm × 26.7 cm) and sort them into eight sets of seven strips each. Stitch these together in sevens, alternating the lighter and darker fabrics (see picture 1). Press seams then trim the sides of each piece straight and cut them across the strips to make four pieces, each 2½ in (6.4 cm) wide (see picture 2).

Now make up four pieces of chequerboard patchwork by taking one piece from each set and sewing them

41

together across the squares, matching seams. Each piece has 56 squares and comprises one quarter of the quilt top (excluding the border). Press the seams then stitch the four pieces together keeping the dark/light chequerboard effect (see picture 3).

THE BORDER

Cut four lengths of the border fabric, each 2½ in (6.4 cm) wide and the correct lengths to fit the top, bottom and sides. From contrasting scraps cut four 2½ in (6.4 cm) squares. Attach the border strips to the top and bottom of the patchwork. Sew a 2½ in (6.4 cm) square to each end of the remaining strips and stitch these to each side of the patchwork, matching seams at the corners (see picture 4). Press seams then press the quilt top on the front.

QUILTING AND FINISHING

On a flat surface, smooth the backing, batting and quilt top together leaving 1 in (2.5 cm) surplus on the backing and batting all round the edge.

Pin the three layers together and baste in a 4 in (10.2 cm) grid, then round the outside edge, making sure there are no tucks or pleats in the front or back. Quilt diagonally across the squares by hand or machine. Stitch the three layers together close to the edges and trim away excess backing and batting.

BINDING

Measure the perimeter of the quilt and cut enough straight-grain binding strips 2½ in (6.4 cm) wide to go round, joining where necessary and allowing about 6 in (15.2 cm) extra for corner mitres. Press seams open then fold the binding in half lengthwise, right sides outwards, and press. Pin the binding to the edges of the quilt on the right sides with all raw edges together. Stitch the binding to the quilt, mitring the corners (see Chapter 1). Turn the binding over to the wrong side, pin down enclosing all raw edges and hem along the stitching line.

1 Strips stitched together in sevens.

2 Strips cut across.

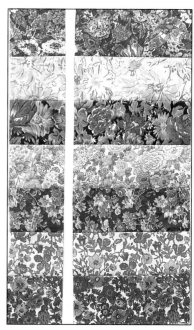

3 Strips reassembled to form chequerboard effect.

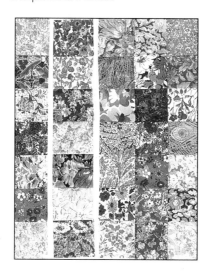

4 Pinning the strips together.

5 Border and corner squares.

THE DOLL'S QUILT

. . . .

The finished size is 15 in × 13 in

(38.1 cm × 33 cm).

MATERIALS REQUIRED
▶ Scraps in cotton dress-weight fabrics
▶ Piece of low-loft wadding: 16 in × 14 in (40.6 cm × 35.6 cm)
▶ Piece of cotton for backing: 16 in × 14 in (40.6 cm × 35.6 cm)

To scale down the crib quilt, cut 30 strips 1½ in (3.8 cm) × 8 in (20.3 cm). Sort them into six sets of five, and make five pieces of strip patchwork each with six strips (see picture 1). Cut each one into 1½ in (3.8 cm) widths across the strips and reassemble into four quarters, each with 30 squares (see pictures 2 and 3). Stitch the four quarters and add a border 1½ in (3.8 cm) wide with corner squares.

Back and interline with the low-loft wadding and quilt by hand or machine. Instead of adding a separate binding, fold the backing over to the front to neaten with a narrow border (see diagram on next page).

1 Strips cut for the doll's quilt.

2 The strips cut and reassembled.

3 1 quarter.

Doll's quilt

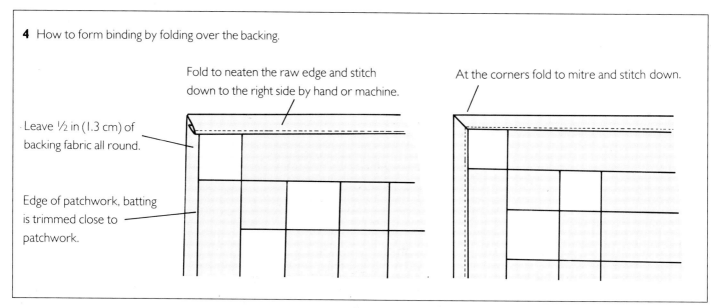

4 How to form binding by folding over the backing.

Fold to neaten the raw edge and stitch down to the right side by hand or machine.

At the corners fold to mitre and stitch down.

Leave ½ in (1.3 cm) of backing fabric all round.

Edge of patchwork, batting is trimmed close to patchwork.

PENCIL OR SEWING-KIT CASE

. . . .

This case is ideal for storing pencils or carrying your sewing kit to classes or on holiday. Make it in these bright colours or devise your own colour scheme. The finished size is approximately 11 in × 7 in (27.9 cm × 15.2 cm).

MATERIALS REQUIRED

Use cotton dress-weight fabric, 44 in (112 cm) wide

▶ Green, red, purple: one piece of each colour 12 in × 4 in (30.5 cm × 10.2 cm)

▶ Yellow: ¼ yd (¼ metre)

▶ 14 squares in plain colours, each 3¼ in (8.2 cm) square

▶ 10–in (25–cm) zipper

I Making the triangle points.

Cut the squares.

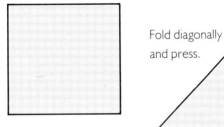

Fold diagonally and press.

Fold again; all raw edges are now together.

Making the triangle points.

2 Pinning on triangle points.

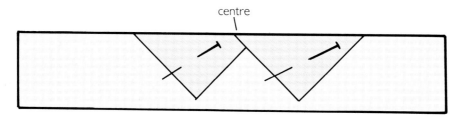

centre

Pin two triangles to the bottom strip.

Pin two points to the first (green) strip.

3 Adding second strip.

Lay another strip on top. Stitch the two strips together, trapping triangles in the seam.

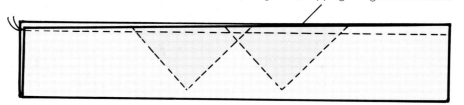

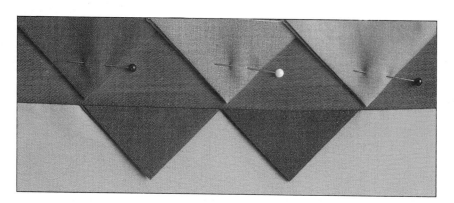

Sew on the second strip trapping the triangle points in the seam.

4 Lining and top strip folded down.

fold

Top-stitch close to seam through all thicknesses.

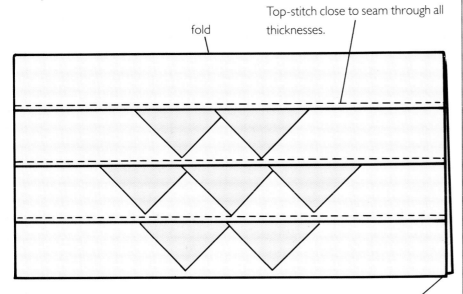

Raw edges are together.

The large rectangle forms the top strip . . .

. . . and lining

CUTTING OUT

All measurements include a ¼ in (6 mm) seam allowance.

From the green, red and purple cut two pieces, each 2 in × 12 in (5.1 cm × 30.5 cm). From the yellow cut two pieces, each 12 in × 8 in (30.5 cm × 20.3 cm). Cut 14 squares, each 3¼ in (8.2 cm) in plain colours.

MAKING THE POINTS

Fold the small squares of fabric diagonally across once, press with a hot iron, then diagonally across again so you have a folded triangle with all raw edges together (see diagram 1).

MAKING UP THE CASE

Mark the centre point of each strip. Take a green strip and position two triangles on top, all raw edges together and pin on the triangles (see diagram 2). Then place the red strip on top, right side down, pin and stitch, taking ¼ in (6 mm) seam allowance and trapping the triangle edges in the seam (see diagram 3). Fold the red strip upwards, pin three triangles along the top edge, then place and pin the purple strip on top and stitch as before. Fold the purple strip upwards and pin two more triangles along the top edge.

Take the large yellow rectangle which will form the top strip and the lining. Pin it to the purple strip, trapping the triangles as before, and stitch. On the wrong side press all the seams towards the yellow piece then fold this over, placing the raw edges together (see diagram 4). Press firmly and top stitch just above the seams through all layers. Repeat for the other side of the case.

Finished pencil case.

5 Insert the zipper before sewing the final seams.

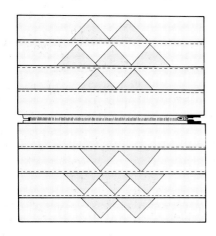

INSERTING THE ZIPPER AND FINISHING

Lay the two sides on a flat surface, right sides uppermost, folded edges together, and insert the zipper in the centre. Stitch in using a zipper foot (see diagram 5).

Fold the case right sides together, pin and stitch down the sides through four thicknesses and along the bottom, being careful not to trap the points in the seam. Trim seams and zigzag-stitch to neaten the inside. Turn right side out and press.

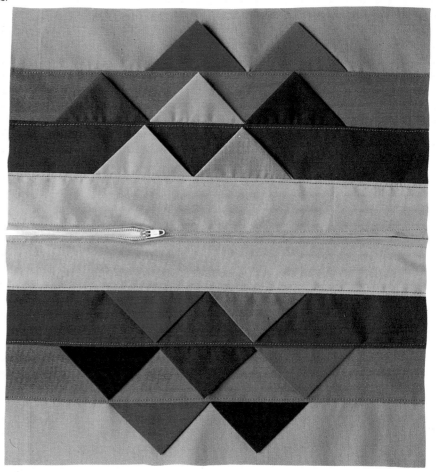

CARD TRICK SHOULDER BAG

· · · · · · · · ·

This simple shoulder bag uses the "Card Trick" block which gives an intriguing optical illusion of shapes folded over each other. Only two templates are needed: a large and a small half-square triangle. The finished block size is 12 in × 12 in (30.5 cm × 30.5 cm).

MATERIALS REQUIRED
Based on 44 in (112 cm) fabric.
▶ Small pieces in three contrasting fabrics
▶ 2–oz batting: 14 in × 28 in (35 cm × 71 cm)
▶ Lining: ½ yd (½ metre)
▶ Binding and straps: ¼ yd (¼ metre)

MAKING THE BLOCK
Draw the block full-size (see diagram 1) and make templates as outlined in Chapter 1. Make one large triangle A and one small triangle B.

From the large triangle A cut four of each three colours (12 triangles). From the small triangle B cut four of each colour also (12 triangles).

Arrange the patches on a flat surface. Join the small triangles then make up the squares with the large triangles.

Make the centre square with four small triangles and the corner squares with eight large triangles (see diagram 3). Join the squares into strips and finally join these to make the block. Make two blocks.

Cut pieces of lining and batting slightly larger than the block and sandwich the batting between the patchwork and the lining. Pin the three layers together and baste in a grid about 4 in (10 cm) apart. Baste around the outer edge. Quilt by hand or machine around the main shapes ¼ in (6 mm) from the seams. Trim the lining and batting to the size of the block.

THE BINDING AND STRAPS

Cut three pieces of binding 2½ in × 12½ in (6.4 cm × 31.6 cm), fold in half lengthways (wrong sides together) and press. Take a length of binding and place the raw edges against one side (the top) of the block on the back and stitch down taking ¼ in (6 mm) seam allowance. Turn the binding over to the right side and stitch down through all thicknesses. Repeat with the other block. These bound edges will form the open, top edges of the bag.

Now baste the two bottom edges of the blocks together and using the third piece of binding repeat, fastening the two blocks together at the bottom edge. Trim the binding to the edges of the blocks and baste the bag together at the two side edges.

Cut two more pieces of binding 2½ in × 36 in (6.4 cm × 91 cm), fold in half lengthwise and press as before. Neaten both ends by turning the raw edges in. Bind the edges of the bag together, extending the stitching along the binding to form straps. Knot the two ends together to adjust length.

I The block showing templates and seams.

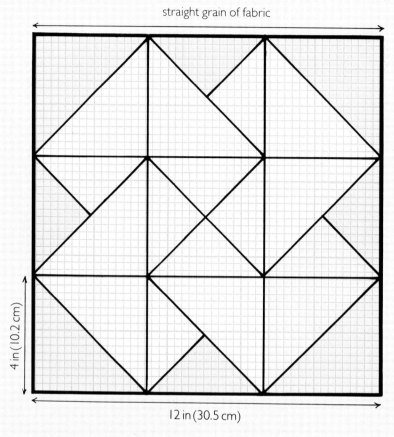

straight grain of fabric

4 in (10.2 cm)

12 in (30.5 cm)

2 The arrangement of colours in the block.

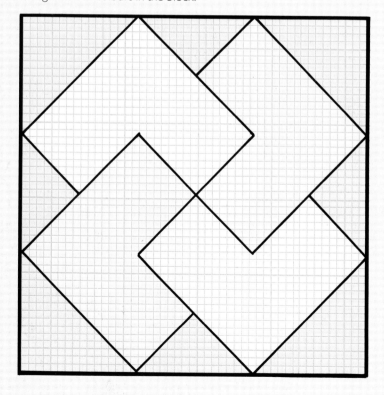

3 Construction order for Card trick block.

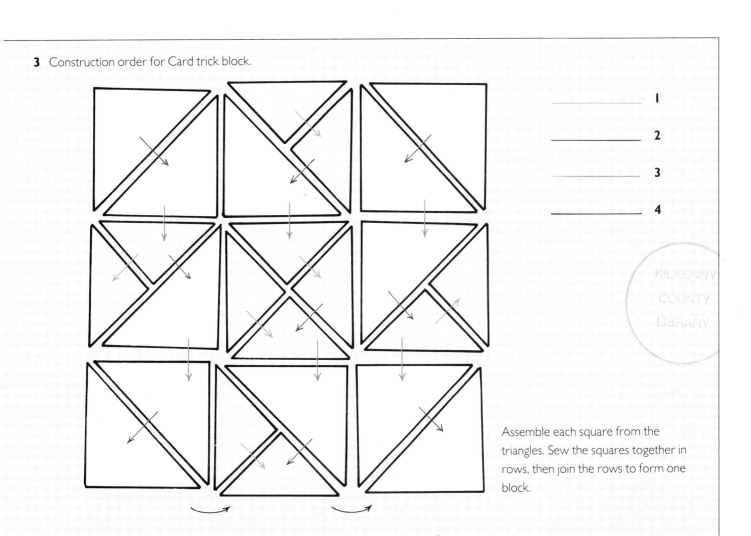

		1
		2
		3
		4

Assemble each square from the triangles. Sew the squares together in rows, then join the rows to form one block.

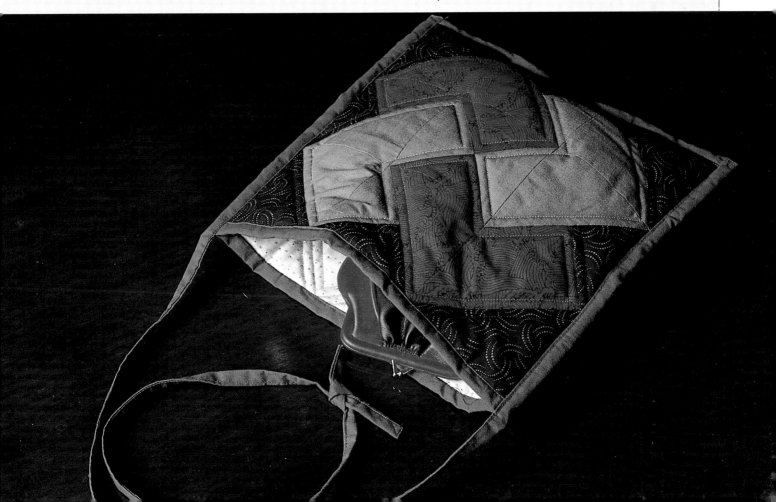

FOLDED STAR STATIONERY FOLDER

· · · · · · · · · · · · ·

The decorative panel on the front

of this stationery folder is made in

"Folded Star", sometimes known

as Somerset Patchwork. The

finished size of the panel is 5 in

(12.7 cm) square.

MATERIALS REQUIRED

Based on 44 in (112 cm) fabric.

► For the folder and lining in dark maroon: 1 yd (1 metre)
► For the star points: small pieces in dark red and pale grey
► For the frame and ties: strip of green 30 in × 2 in (76.2 cm × 5.1 cm)
► White cotton: 6 in (15.2 cm) square
► Piece of cartridge paper: 30 in × 25 in (76 cm × 63 cm) (approximate size)
► Two pieces of card: 10 in × 8 in (25.4 cm × 20.3 cm)

MAKING THE FOLDED STAR PANEL

The white cotton is cut 6 in (15.2 cm) square (ie a little larger all round than the panel) to allow for trimming to size when finished. Mark diagonal, horizontal and vertical lines on the square.

For the star points, cut 20 pieces of red, 1¼ in × 2 in (3.2 cm × 5.1 cm). Cut 24 pieces of grey, 1¼ in × 2 in (3.2 cm × 5.1 cm).

Turn in and press a ¼ in (6 mm) hem along one long side of each piece (see diagram 1). Crease a line down the centre of each piece (see diagram 2). Then fold corners down to make star points (see diagram 3).

In the centre of the 6 in (15.2 cm) square of white cotton place four red star points with the folded gap uppermost.

Secure the points down to the backing with a stitch in matching thread. Baste the outer raw edges to the backing (see diagram 4).

Now place and pin a second ring of eight star points in grey, ½ in (1.3 mm) from centre, and secure as before with matching thread (see diagram 5). The third ring is in red. To square up the design, place two points at the top, bottom and sides and one at each corner (see diagram 6). The fourth ring in grey has three points at the top, bottom and sides and one at each corner. Finally, place and secure a red point at each corner (see diagram 7).

Cut four strips of green 1½ in × 5½ in (3.8 cm × 14 cm), fold (wrong sides together) and press in half lengthwise. Place the folded strips around the outer

---

Star points   **1** Folding down the hem.   **2** Creasing the centre.

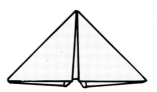

3 Folding down the corners.

4 Attaching the first round of four star points.

5 The second ring of eight points.

edges of the star panel to frame it and stitch down to the backing, inside the fold. Press the panel and trim to 5 in (12.7 cm) square.

MAKING THE PAPER PATTERN FOR THE FOLDER

The pattern measurements have ¼ in (6 mm) seam allowance included.

From the paper measure and cut the following pieces:

1. 5 in × 2½ in (12.7 cm × 6.4 cm)
2. 5 in × 4 in (12.7 cm × 10.2 cm)
3. 10½ in × 2 in (26.7 cm × 5.1 cm)
4. 9 in × 10½ in (22.9 cm × 26.7 cm)
5. 4 in × 5½ in (10.2 cm × 14 cm) for the pen pocket
6. 4½ in × 8 in (11.4 cm × 20.3 cm) for the stamps/address book pocket
7. Wedge-shaped flap with measurements

as shown (see diagram 8).

Number each piece. On piece 7, mark a dot at the mid-point of the long straight side for the tie position.

Using the pattern pieces 1–6, cut out one piece of each from the fabric. For piece 7 (the flaps), cut two.

THE TIES

For the ties cut two strips of the green fabric 1¾ in × 9 in (4.4 cm × 22.9 cm). Fold in half lengthwise (right sides together) and stitch the long sides. Trim the seam to ³⁄₁₆ in (5 mm). Press the seam open and stitch across on the short end, then turn inside out and press again.

THE POCKETS

Fold the pen pocket (piece 5) lengthwise (right sides together) and stitch along the

long side. Press the seam open and stitch across the base, placing the seam in the centre. Turn inside out and press, tuck in ¼ in (6 mm) at the top to neaten the raw edges and stitch to close the gap. Fold piece 6 widthwise and repeat as for piece 5. The pockets are now double so there is no need to turn edges in or hem when stitching to the folder.

MAKING THE FOLDER

Diagram 9 shows the construction of the folder.

Take the Folded Star panel and stitch piece 1 to the top and piece 2 to the bottom. Press seams towards the top and bottom edges. Now add pieces 3 and 4 to the sides and press seams outwards. Stitch the raw edges of the ties to the points marked on the flaps. Then add the flaps

6 The third ring of points and squaring up the design.

7 The fourth ring of points and the corner points.

8 The wedge-shaped flap template.

The wedge-shaped flap (piece 7) with measurements and tie position.

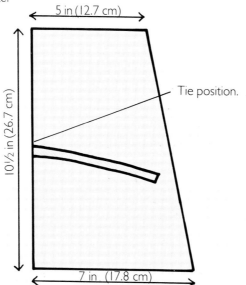

5 in (12.7 cm)

10½ in (26.7 cm)

Tie position.

7 in (17.8 cm)

(piece 7) to the sides, placing the wider base of the wedge at the bottom and trapping the ties in the seams. Press these seams open. Top stitch round the panel close to the seam.(The two pockets, pieces 5 and 6, are added at the next stage.)

THE LINING

Place the remaining fabric right side uppermost on a flat surface. Place the folder on top, right side down. Smooth together, pin and stitch round the edges, leaving an opening between the arrows (see diagram 9). (N.B. Be careful at this point not to trap the ties in the seams.) Trim seams and corners, turn to the right side and press, turning ¼ in (6 mm) in on both sides of the opening. Stitch down the seams between the flaps and folder and down the fold line which is half-way between these seams. This forms the casings for the card stiffeners. Position the pockets on the flaps and stitch firmly. Cut two pieces of card to fit the front and back, each 7 in × 9½ in (17.8 cm × 24.2 cm), and slide through the gaps at the base of the folder. Baste the opening together then fold the flaps over at the seams, pin down and stitch firmly across the top and bottom through all thicknesses.

9 The construction of the folder.

Fold line.

Top-stitch close to seams.

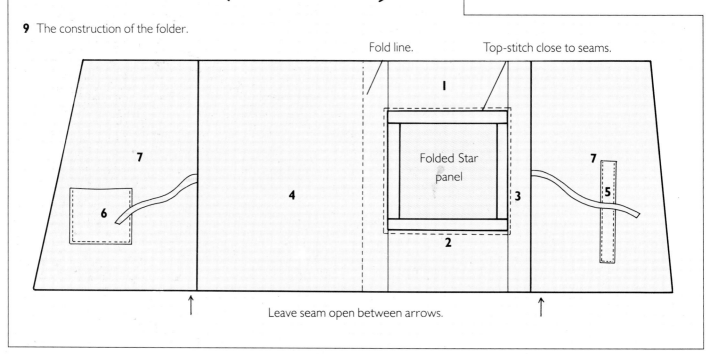

Leave seam open between arrows.

JEWELLERY TRAVELLING CASE

· · · · · · · · · ·

Keep valuables safe in this neat jewellery roll when you go on holiday. The patchwork design used is the "Flying Geese" pattern taken from a traditional patchwork block. The finished size when open is 13 in × 7 in (33 cm × 17.8 cm).

MATERIALS REQUIRED

▶ For the triangles and binding: small pieces of plain fabric in four colours
▶ For the lining, ties and background triangles: ¼ yd (¼ metre) in another plain colour
▶ 5-in (12.7-cm) zipper
▶ One small button

THE PATCHWORK PANEL

(All measurements include a ¼ in (6 mm) seam allowance.)

Using the measurements given make templates for large triangle A and small triangle B (see diagram 1). A seam allowance of ¼ in (6 mm) must be added either to the templates or when cutting out fabrics (see Chapter 1, Making Templates). Using triangle A, cut 8 blue

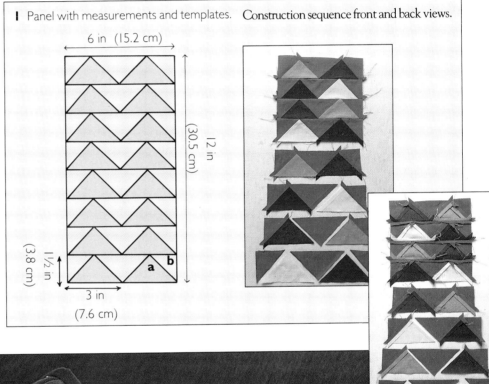

I Panel with measurements and templates. Construction sequence front and back views.

6 in (15.2 cm)

12 in (30.5 cm)

1½ in (3.8 cm)

a b

3 in (7.6 cm)

and 16 in the other colours. Using triangle B, cut 16 blue.

Piece triangles together in strips, each with a blue central triangle A (see diagram 2), then stitch the strips together to form the patchwork panel 6 in × 12 in (15.2 cm × 30.5 cm).

Cut the batting and lining 14 in × 8 in (35.6 cm × 20.3 cm) and sandwich the batting between the patchwork and lining. Pin and baste, then quilt by hand or machine. Stitch all round the outside close to the edges and trim the lining and batting to the same size as the patchwork.

THE POCKET

From the lining fabric cut two pieces:
(a) 2 in × 7 in (5.1 cm × 17.8 cm)
(b) 14 in × 7 in (35.6 cm × 17.8 cm).
Fold piece (b) in half (wrong sides together) to form a 7 in (17.8 cm) square. Fold piece (a) in half lengthwise (right sides together), stitch down the long side, turn inside out and press. Insert the zipper between piece (a) and (b) by placing the fold of piece (b) against the zipper (see diagram 3).

Place the pocket against the back of the lined patchwork panel and baste round the three outside edges. Stitch down piece (a) along the fold.

THE RING KEEP

From the lining fabric cut a strip 7 in × 2¼ in (17.8 cm × 5.7 cm). Fold in half lengthwise (right sides together), stitch down the long side and turn inside out to form a tube.

Cut a strip of batting 1½ in × 7 in (3.8 cm × 17.8 cm) and thread this through the tube. Turn in the raw edges on one end and slip hem to neaten. Pin the tube to the edge of the panel so the neatened end is 1 in (2.5 cm) from the other side (see diagram 4).

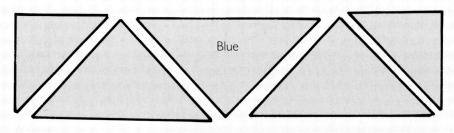

The patchwork panel quilted onto batting and backing.

2 Piecing triangles in strips.

Blue

3 Stitching zipper between pocket pieces.

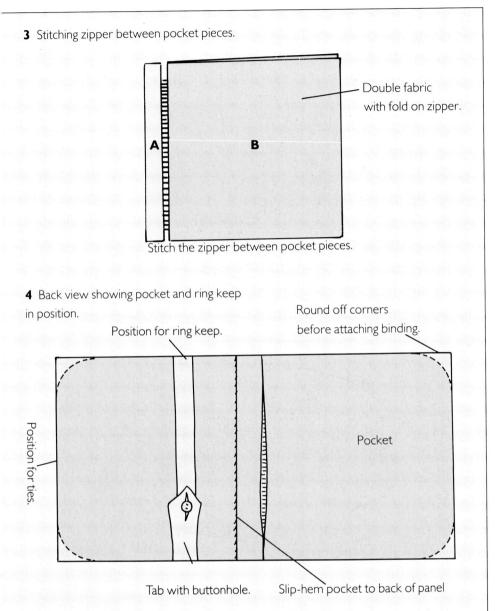

Double fabric with fold on zipper.

Stitch the zipper between pocket pieces.

4 Back view showing pocket and ring keep in position.

Position for ring keep.

Round off corners before attaching binding.

Position for ties.

Pocket

Tab with buttonhole.

Slip-hem pocket to back of panel

5 Making the tab.

Sew in half, press seam open at centre back, then stitch across one end in a point. Trim seams, turn inside out and press.

THE TAB

Cut a piece from the lining fabric 2½ in × 2½ in (6.4 cm × 6.4 cm). Fold in half (right sides together) and stitch seam. Press seam open then stitch across one end to form a point (see diagram 5). Trim seams, turn inside out and press. Make a buttonhole at the end of the tab and pin opposite the tube on the panel so that it overlaps by 1 in (2.5 cm). Stitch the button to the end of the tube.

THE TIES

From the lining fabric cut two strips 2½ in × 10 in (6.4 cm × 25.4 cm). Make ties by folding right sides together, stitching the long sides then across one end. Turn inside out and press. Pin ties onto the right side of the panel in the centre of the short end nearest the tab. Round off corners through all thicknesses.

BINDING

Cut a piece of bias binding 36 in × 2 in (91.4 cm × 5.1 cm), seaming together where necessary. Sew into a ring then fold in half (wrong sides together) and press. Pin and baste the raw edges of binding to the right sides of the panel. Stitch through all thicknesses, catching in the pocket edges, ring keep and tab and ties. Fold the bias binding over to the back and slip hem all round.

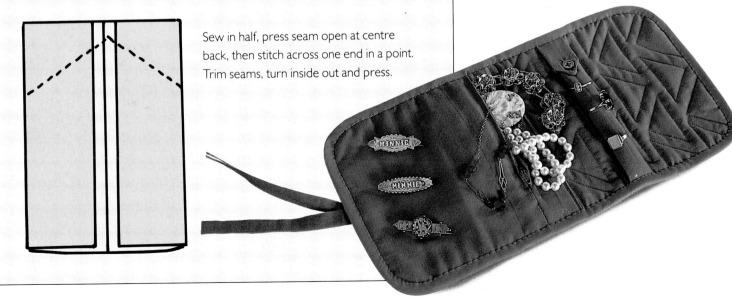

SPECTACLE CASE WITH SEMINOLE PATCHWORK

. . . .

This ingenious form of patchwork was developed by the Seminole Indians of Florida, hence its name. Long strips of different coloured fabrics are first stitched together, then cut and reassembled in a variety of intricate designs with the characteristic small geometric shapes. The finished size is 8 in × 10 in (20.2 cm × 25.4 cm).

MATERIALS REQUIRED

Choose contrasting fabrics. Traditionally, plain fabrics are used but small prints are also effective.

▶ For the patchwork: small pieces in red, pink, turquoise and green
▶ Pelmet vilene: 8 in (20.3 cm) sq.
▶ Lining: cotton fabric 9 in × 12 in (22.9 cm × 30.5 cm)
▶ One sheet of A4-size paper in a good, firm quality

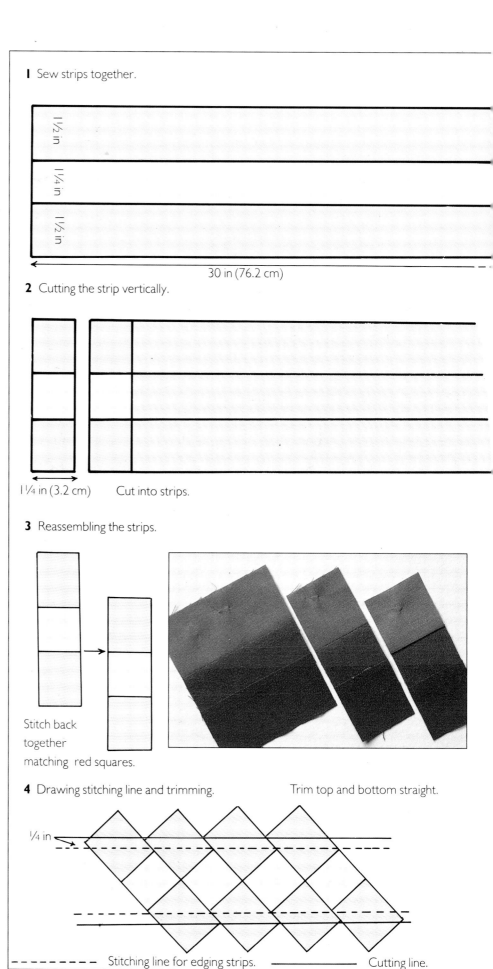

1 Sew strips together.

1½ in

1¼ in

1½ in

30 in (76.2 cm)

2 Cutting the strip vertically.

1¼ in (3.2 cm)   Cut into strips.

3 Reassembling the strips.

Stitch back together matching red squares.

4 Drawing stitching line and trimming.   Trim top and bottom straight.

¼ in

- - - - Stitching line for edging strips.   ———— Cutting line.

Alternate strips can be reversed to give this variation.

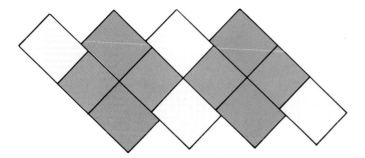

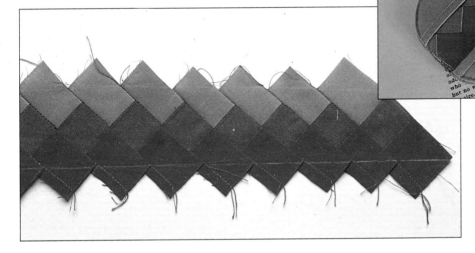

5 Adding green borders to the Seminole strip.

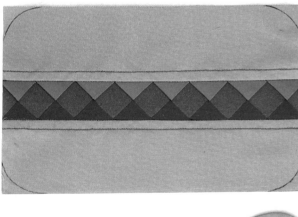

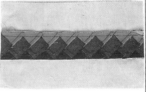

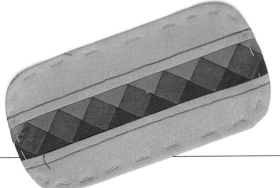

MAKING THE SEMINOLE STRIPS

All measurements include seam allowances of ¼ in (6 mm).

In turquoise and pink, cut one strip of each 1½ in × 30 in (3.8 cm × 76.2 cm) (on the straight grain). In red cut one strip 1¼ in × 30 in (3.2 cm × 76.2 cm).

Seam the three together with the red in the centre (see diagram 1). Press the seams to one side on the back and press again on the front, making sure there are no tucks at the seams.

Now cut this strip into pieces 1¼ in (3.2 cm) wide (see diagram 2). For each side of the case stitch nine pieces together, dropping the seams as in diagram 3. With a fabric marker draw a straight line across the corners of the red squares on either side then add ¼ in (6 mm) seam allowance beyond this line and trim away the excess (see diagram 4). Straighten the short edges. For each strip cut two pieces of the green fabric 2½ in × 9 in (6.4 cm × 22.9 cm) and stitch either side of the Seminole strip, taking the ¼ in (6 mm) seam allowance (see diagram 5). Press seams towards the green on the back and top stitch ¼ in (6 mm) from the seams on the right side.

MAKING THE CASE

Trace the case template (see diagram 6) and cut out two pieces of pelmet vilene and two pieces of paper. Place a piece of vilene on the wrong side of the patchwork, positioning the patchwork in the centre of the vilene. Adjust so the top and bottom coincide with the points of a red square (see picture). Cut round the outside of the patchwork, rounding off the corners and allowing ½ in (1.3 cm) to turn over the back of the vilene. Run a gathering thread round the curves and pull up to create a smooth curve which fits closely round the vilene. Baste the patchwork to the vilene.

THE LINING

Cut two pieces of lining fabric ½ in (1.3 cm) larger than the paper shapes and gather the curved edges. Pin the papers to the wrong side of the lining, pull up gathers and baste fabric to paper (see diagram 7). Steam press to form a firm crease. Now carefully remove the basting stitching and paper and pin the lining onto the back of the case, wrong sides together. Slip hem the lining to the case all the way round, edges together (see diagram 8). Repeat for the other side. On each side, top stitch over the curve as far as the dots on the template, then place the two sides of the case together and stitch through all thicknesses, reinforcing with a back-stitch at the opening.

6 Template for the case.

7 Making the lining round a paper template.

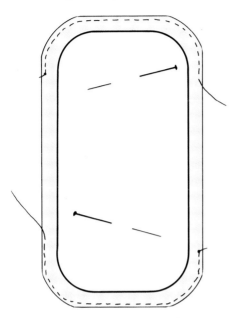

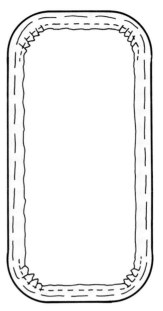

Pin paper to the wrong side of the lining fabric. Cut fabric ½ in (1.3 cm) larger all round than the paper. Gather the curved edges.

Pull up the gathers and baste the fabric to the paper. Steam press, then remove the paper carefully, – gathering threads can be left in.

8 Hemming the lining to the case.

9 Place the two sides together and stitch through all thicknesses.

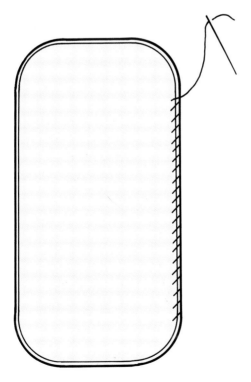

Slip hem the lining to the back of the case.

Top stitch each side of the case between the dots.

CAMERA STRAP

. . . .

Personalize your camera, binoculars or guitar with this strap made in Seminole patchwork. The finished size is length 48 in (122 cm), width 2½ in (6.4 cm).

1 Sewing sequence for the long strips.

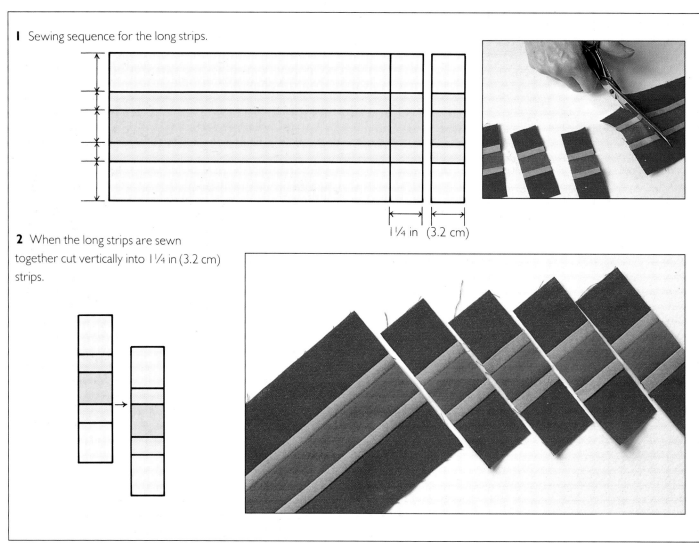

1¼ in (3.2 cm)

2 When the long strips are sewn together cut vertically into 1¼ in (3.2 cm) strips.

3 Align them as illustrated and stitch them together.

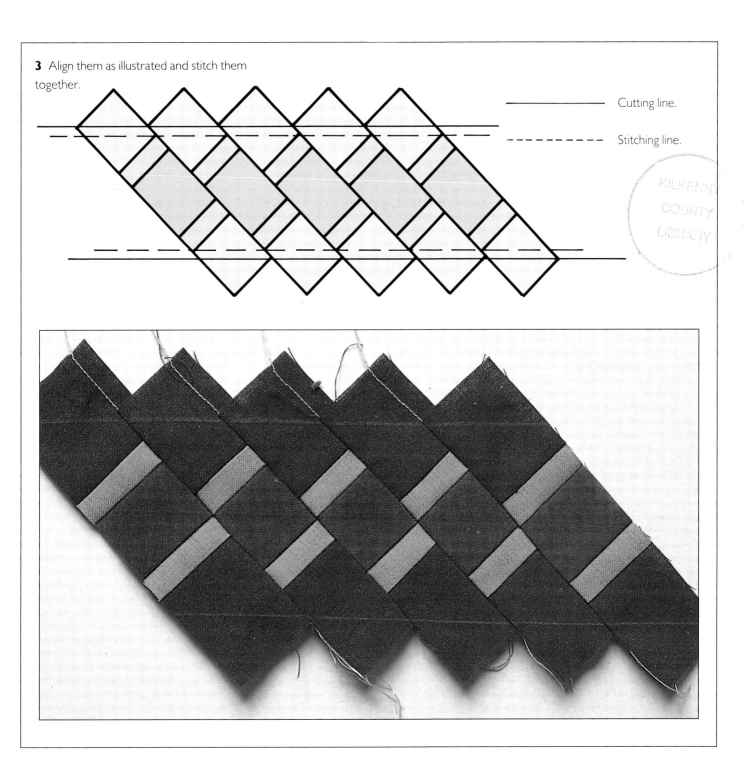

Cutting line.

Stitching line.

MATERIALS REQUIRED

Based on 44 in (112 cm) fabric.

▶ Pink, green and red: ⅛ yd (⅛ metre) of each

▶ Mauve: ¼ yd (¼ metre)

▶ Medium-weight iron-on interfacing: ¼ yd (¼ metre)

▶ 2 bar clips

MAKING THE PATCHWORK

Measurements include a ¼ in (6 mm) seam allowance.

Cut the strips of fabric across the width of the material from selvedge to selvedge so they are 44 in (112 cm) long. Cut two pink 1½ in (3.8 cm) wide, two green ¾ in (1.9 cm) wide, and one red 1¼ in (3.2 cm) wide. Join a green strip to either side of the red strip, then join the mauve strips to the green strips (see diagram 1). Cut vertically into 1¼ in (3.2 cm) wide strips and rejoin, aligning as shown in diagram 2. With a fabric marker, draw stitching lines above the green corners, add on a ¼ in (6 mm) seam allowance beyond these, and cut away the excess (see diagram 3). Make up one length of patchwork approximately 40 in (102 cm). Press well on the back and front.

4 Trim away the excess leaving ¼ in (6 mm) beyond the green corners for the seam allowance.

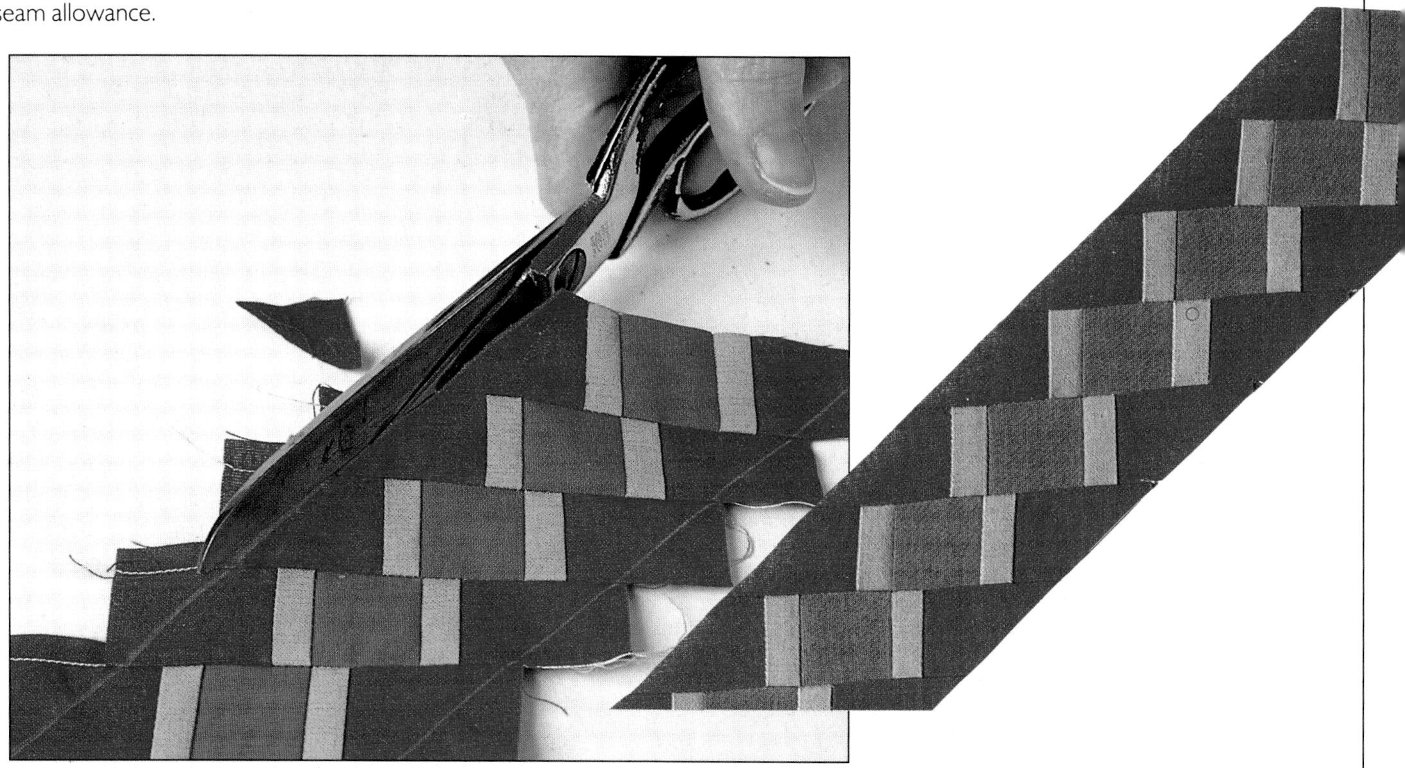

5 Template for the loops.

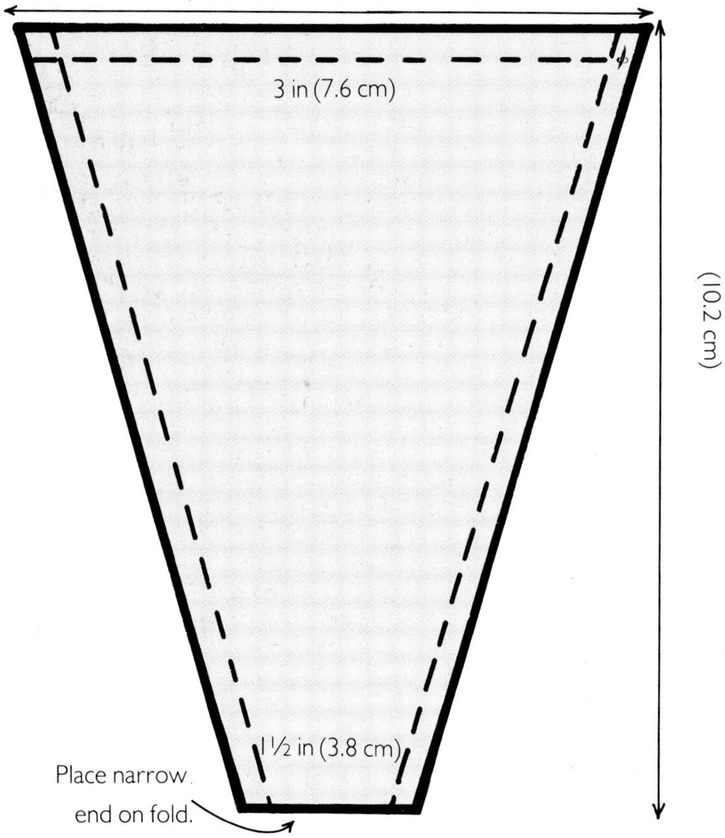

3 in (7.6 cm)

4 in (10.2 cm)

1 ½ in (3.8 cm)

Place narrow end on fold.

6 Making the loop.

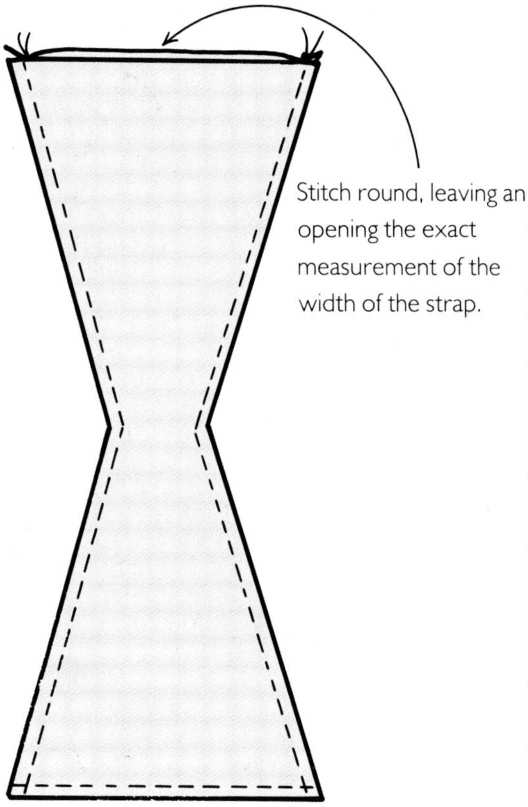

Stitch round, leaving an opening the exact measurement of the width of the strap.

7 Attaching the loop to the ends of the strap.

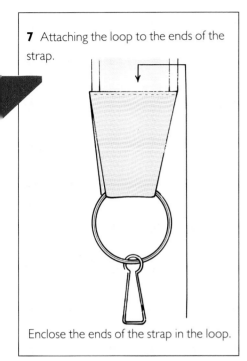

Enclose the ends of the strap in the loop.

THE SIDE STRIPS

Cut the two side strips from the mauve the length of the patchwork and 1½ in (3.8 cm) and 3½ in (8.9 cm) wide respectively. Cut strips of interfacing to fit and iron onto the back of each strip. Now take the narrower strip (1½ in/3.8 cm) and stitch down one side of the patchwork, right sides together, stitching exactly on the seam line. Press seam towards the side (mauve) strip. Mark a line on the side strip ½ in (1.3 cm) from the seam. Fold back on this line and press. Stitch the wider strip down the other side of the patchwork, measure and mark a line ½ in (1.3 cm) from the seam and fold back as before. Neaten the other long side of the second strip by turning in a narrow hem. Now lap this over and hem down.

At each end of the strap, stitch straight across to fasten the layers together.

THE LOOPS

Using the measurements given in diagram 5, cut four pieces of fabric in mauve and two of interfacing. Iron interfacing to the wrong sides of two pieces. Place an interfaced piece and a non-interfaced piece with right sides together and stitch round all except one short edge. Trim seams, turn inside out and press to make shaped loops. Turn in ¼ in (6 mm) on the open end, then enclose the ends of the strap inside the loop and baste through all layers. Stitch firmly across the ends then place purchased bar clip on loop, fold the end up and stitch again through all thicknesses several times across.

OVERNIGHT BAG

. . . .

The patchwork blocks for this travel bag couldn't be simpler, each one made up of only three pieces. The finished bag size is 17 in × 24 in (43.2 cm × 61 cm).

MATERIALS REQUIRED

▶ A mixture of plain and patterned fabric scraps
▶ For the lining: 1 yd (1 metre)
▶ 2–oz batting: 1 yd (1 metre)
▶ Plain fabric for the binding and handles: ½ yd (½ metre)
▶ 1 20–in (50–cm) zipper

THE PATCHWORK BLOCKS

All measurements include a seam allowance of ¼ in (6 mm).

Sort the fabric scraps into dark- and light-colour values. Cut 38 dark strips 8½ in × 3 in (21.6 cm × 7.6 cm) and 19 light strips 8½ in × 3½ in (21.6 cm × 8.9 cm). Join the strips in threes (see diagram 1) and make up 19 blocks.

FRONT AND BACK

Make two panels each of six blocks, 3 × 2 (see diagram 2).

Cut two pieces each of lining and batting 18 in × 26 in (45.7 cm × 66 cm). Sandwich one piece of batting between a patchwork panel and the lining. Smooth flat and pin the three layers together. Baste in a grid about 4 in (10.2 cm) apart

1 A single block.

2 Joining six blocks to make a panel.

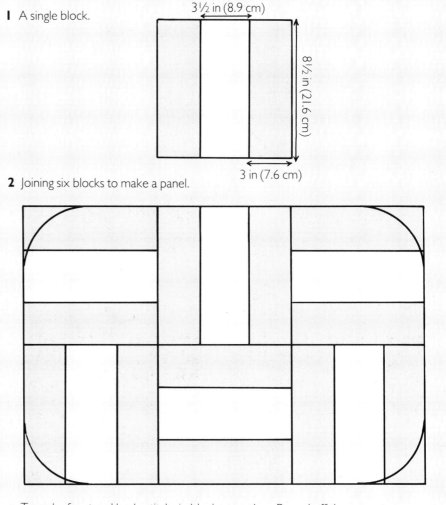

To make front and back, stitch six blocks together. Round off the corners.

then quilt by hand or machine. Round off the corners and stitch the three layers together, close to the edge all round the outside. Trim away the excess batting and lining. Repeat for the other panel.

THE SIDES

Take two more blocks and cut each in half across the strips to make four pieces, 4¼ in × 8½ in (10.8 cm × 21.6 cm). Make two longer strips by joining two pieces together (see diagram 3).

THE BASE

Take another two blocks and cut in half as before, then join three strips to make the base (see diagram 4). Discard the fourth piece. Stitch the side panels to either side of the base, short edges together. Now cut strips of lining and batting 58 in × 5½ in (50 cm × 14 cm), sandwich the batting between the patchwork and lining and quilt the three layers together as for the front and back panels. Stitch close to the raw edges and trim away excess lining and batting.

THE ZIPPER PANEL (TOP OF BAG)

Using the remaining three blocks, cut these in half across the strips and join into two lengths, each 24½ in (62.3 cm). Now trim each of these strips to a width of 2½ in (6.4 cm).

Cut two pieces of lining and batting 26 in × 4 in (66 cm × 10.2 cm). For each side of the zipper panel place a patchwork strip and lining right sides together with the batting strip underneath, pin and stitch along one long side, taking ¼ in (6 mm) seam allowance. Trim away excess batting close to the seam, then turn the patchwork and lining to the outside with the batting inside. Stitch close to the raw edges to fasten the three layers together.

Insert the zipper between the two strips, placing the seamed edges close to the zipper teeth (see diagram 5).

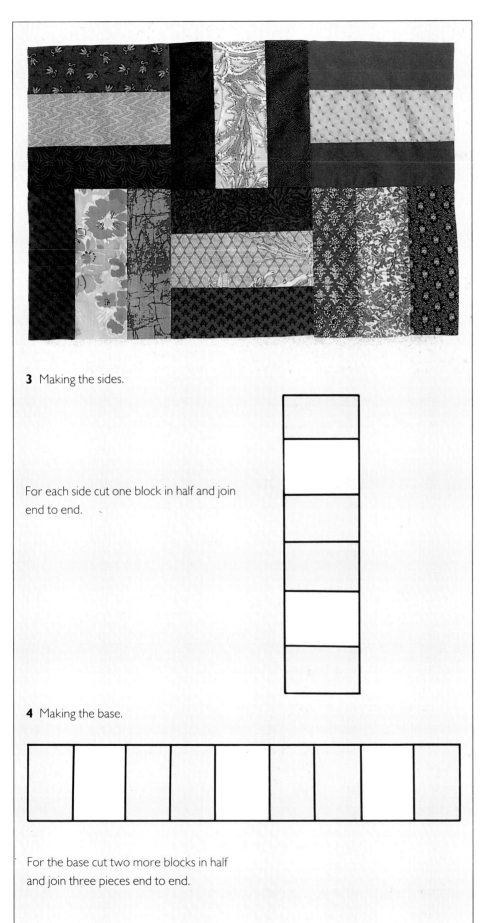

3 Making the sides.

For each side cut one block in half and join end to end.

4 Making the base.

For the base cut two more blocks in half and join three pieces end to end.

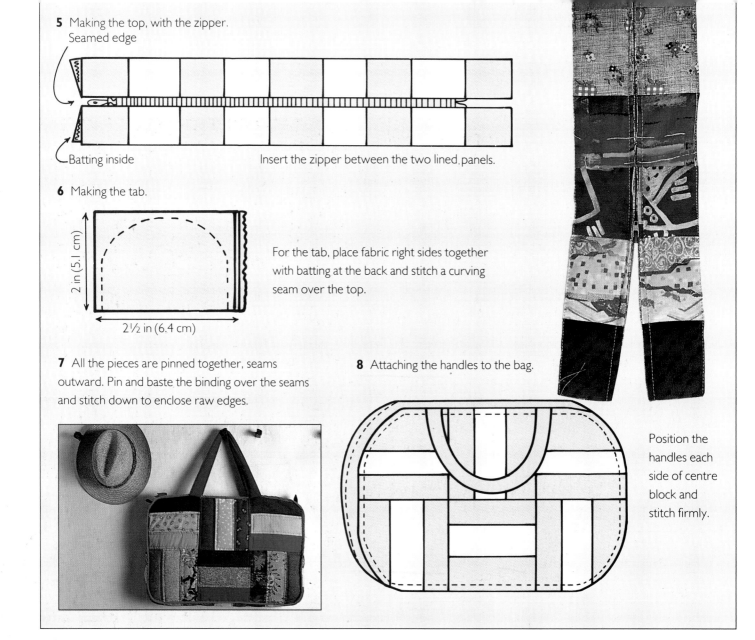

5 Making the top, with the zipper.
Seamed edge

Batting inside

Insert the zipper between the two lined panels.

6 Making the tab.

2 in (5.1 cm)

2½ in (6.4 cm)

For the tab, place fabric right sides together with batting at the back and stitch a curving seam over the top.

7 All the pieces are pinned together, seams outward. Pin and baste the binding over the seams and stitch down to enclose raw edges.

8 Attaching the handles to the bag.

Position the handles each side of centre block and stitch firmly.

THE TABS

For each tab cut two pieces of fabric 2½ in × 2 in (6.4 cm × 5.1 cm) and one piece of batting. Place the fabric pieces right sides together, batting underneath, and stitch together curving the seam over the top (see diagram 6). Trim seams and turn the tabs right sides out, batting inside. Pin tabs to each end of the zipper panel with all raw edges together. Pin and baste each end of the side and base strip to these ends. Stitch through all layers, trapping the tabs in the short seams and making a continuous ring of the top, sides and base. Close gaps at either end of the zipper by oversewing firmly on the back.

ATTACHING FRONT AND BACK PANELS TO THE SIDES

With wrong sides together, pin the front and back panels of the bag to the sides,

base and top, easing to fit round the curved corners.

BINDING

Make up two rings of bias binding 2½ in (6.4 cm) wide, 74 in (188 cm) long, cut from the plain fabric. Fold in half lengthwise and press, trim off any seam allowances which project. Pin and baste the binding to the sides, top and base panel with all raw edges together, fastening the front and back panels of the bag to the sides. Stitch through all thicknesses taking ¼ in (6 mm) seam allowance.

THE HANDLES

From the plain fabric cut two strips 4½ in × 24 in (11.4 cm × 61 cm). Fold in half lengthwise, right sides together, and stitch into a tube. Press seams open then

stitch loosely across the bottom and turn inside out. Unpick end stitching to form an open-ended tube. Cut two lengths of batting 25 in × 4 in (63.5 × 10.2 cm). Attach threads to the ends of the batting and pull through the tubes to form padded handles. Stitch across the ends to secure the batting and trim away excess. Position the handles on the bag either side of the centre block and pin to the seams between the stitching and raw edges (see diagram 8). Stitch the handles firmly to the seam allowance, reinforcing with several rows of stitching. Finally, fold the bias binding over, enclosing the raw edges and stitch down through all layers, again stitching across the ends of the handles several times to reinforce. Make a narrow loop for the zipper pull from the remaining plain fabric.

HEXAGON ROSETTE PIN-CUSHION

. . . .

This pin-cushion made from two hexagon rosettes is a good way of learning to use a window template. The window template enables you to frame a specific part of the fabric you are using in order to centre a motif. The finished size is 4 in (10 cm) across.

MATERIALS REQUIRED

▶ Cotton fabric which has a suitable motif or pattern: ¼ yd (¼ metre) (see picture)

▶ A piece of stiff card A4–size

▶ Good-quality paper A4–size: 2 sheets

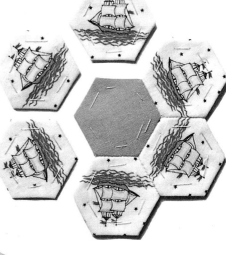

MAKING THE HEXAGONS

Trace the template and make one out of stiff card (see diagram 1). The centre shape is the one used to make your papers. Cut 14 papers. Place the "window" over the chosen motif in the fabric and draw round the outside line (see diagram 2). This is the cutting line and allows enough fabric to turn over when basting the fabric patches onto the papers. Cover the papers using the method described for the Hexagonal Mosaic Pillow, pp 34–36.

Stitch seven hexagons together into a rosette, with one in the centre and six attached around it (see diagram 3). Make a second rosette and press each one.

MAKING UP

Place the two rosettes right sides together and stitch round the outer edges, leaving a gap for stuffing. Remove the basting-stitches and papers then turn right sides out and stuff firmly before neatly closing the gap.

1 Window template.

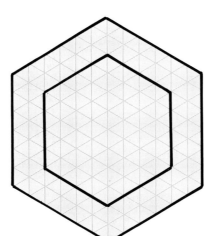

2 Drawing round the template.

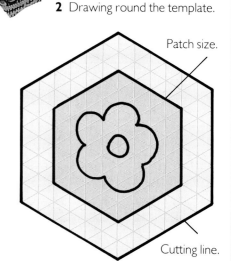

Patch size.

Cutting line.

Centring a motif using a window template.

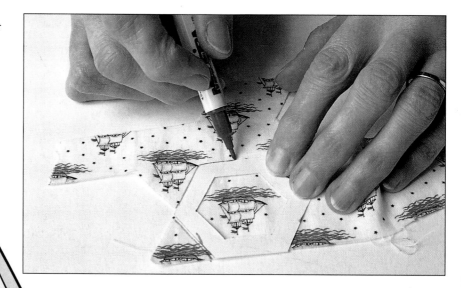

3 Joining the hexagons.

Join the centre patch to one of the side patches then, adding a third patch, stitch up the sides with the same thread. Rejoin the thread to the centre patch and continue along the second side and up the side. Continue until all hexagons are joined.

4 Making the rosettes.

FRUIT BASKET BLOCK

. . . .

There is no reason why patchwork
and quilting should not be purely
decorative and this Fruit Basket
block is designed to be framed. The
basket block is a traditional
favourite, combining patchwork
and appliqué. First make up the
basket in pieced patchwork, then
add fruit or flowers in appliqué.
Final details such as stalks and
small leaves can be embroidered.
The finished size of the block is
15 in (38 cm) square.

MATERIALS REQUIRED

▶ Two contrasting fabrics for the
basket: ¼ yd (¼ metre) of each
▶ Scraps of fabric for the appliqué
▶ Batting: 16 in (40.6 cm) square
▶ Lining: 16 in (40.6 cm) square
▶ Good-quality paper: 2 or 3 A4–
size sheets

THE BASKET

Make a triangle and a square template,
based on a 2 in (5.1 cm) grid. Piece the
block centre first (see diagram 1). Turn to

1 The templates and the block centre.

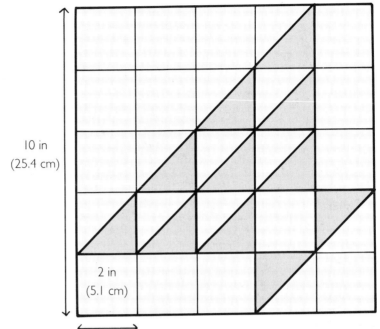

10 in
(25.4 cm)

2 in
(5.1 cm)

Make up the block centre with the basket motif.

2 Adding the corners.

Set the centre on point and add corners.

set this on the bottom point and add the corners (see diagram 2). Press the block on the back and front.

THE FRUIT

Make the templates for the fruit shapes from the paper (see diagram 3). For each shape place the template onto the wrong side of the fabric and cut out, allowing approximately ¼ in (6 mm) seam allowance. Run a gathering thread around the outside of the rounded shapes and pull up to fit the fabric against the paper in a smooth curve (see diagram 4). Fasten off the gathering thread and steam press to give the shapes a sharp-creased edge.

Remove the paper template and position the shapes onto the block and stitch down with a neat hemming-stitch. Build up the fruit shapes, overlapping some to give a realistic appearance to the block (see diagram 5). Small details can be embroidered on by hand or machine.

3 Templates for the fruit shapes.

4 Making the fruit shapes in fabric.

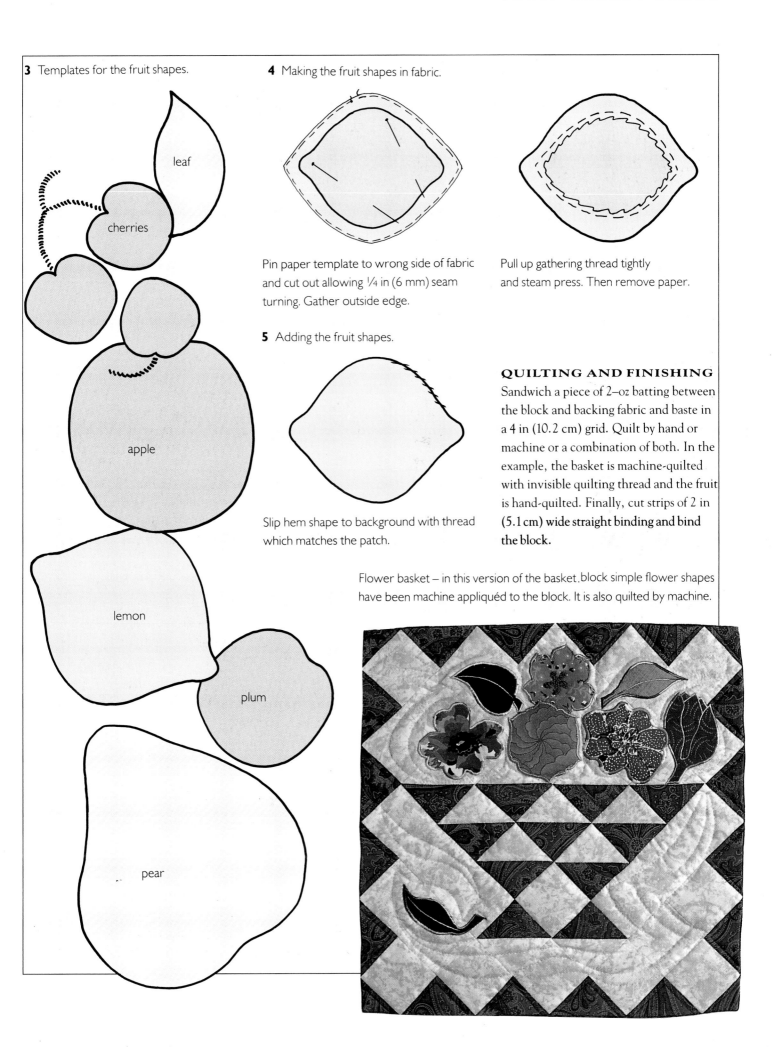

Pin paper template to wrong side of fabric and cut out allowing ¼ in (6 mm) seam turning. Gather outside edge.

Pull up gathering thread tightly and steam press. Then remove paper.

5 Adding the fruit shapes.

Slip hem shape to background with thread which matches the patch.

QUILTING AND FINISHING
Sandwich a piece of 2–oz batting between the block and backing fabric and baste in a 4 in (10.2 cm) grid. Quilt by hand or machine or a combination of both. In the example, the basket is machine-quilted with invisible quilting thread and the fruit is hand-quilted. Finally, cut strips of 2 in **(5.1 cm) wide straight binding and bind the block.**

Flower basket – in this version of the basket.block simple flower shapes have been machine appliquéd to the block. It is also quilted by machine.

CATHEDRAL WINDOW PATCHWORK

. . . .

This intriguing form of patchwork is made by first folding and stitching base squares of fabric which, when sewn together, form a frame for the decorative squares of fabric in the "window". Try out the technique with this simple pin-cushion which requires only two base squares and, if you feel inspired, experiment with a decorative panel like the one illustrated. The finished size of the pin-cushion is 4 in (10.2 cm) square.

MATERIALS REQUIRED

▶ Two squares of plain fabric: 8½ in (21.6 cm)

▶ Two squares of patterned fabric: 2¼ in (5.7 cm)

▶ A small amount of soft toy stuffing

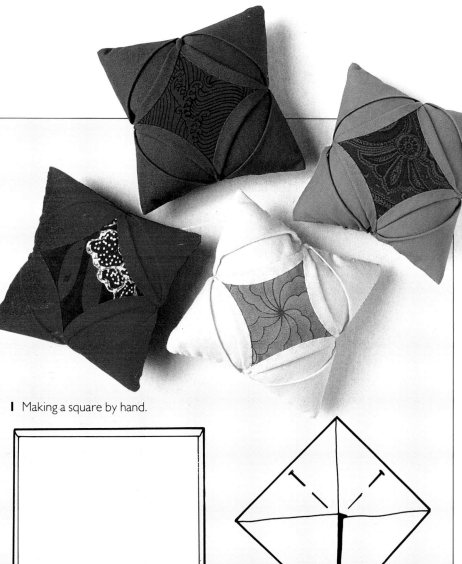

1 Making a square by hand.

a Turn a narrow hem and press. Find the centre point of the square.

b Turn the corners to the centre point and pin down. Press again to crease the outer fold.

c Fold the corners to the centre again.

d Stitch across the centre to fasten the corners down through all thicknesses.

MAKING UP

Follow diagram 1 for hand sewing or diagram 2 for machine sewing, and prepare two squares.

Sew the two squares together then stitch one of the patterned squares into the frame (see diagram 3).

Make a tube by placing opposite edges right sides together and oversew. Turn inside out and stitch in the second patterned square, then whipstitch across the top opening neatly. Repeat across the bottom opening, stuffing firmly before closing the gap.

2 Making a square by machine.

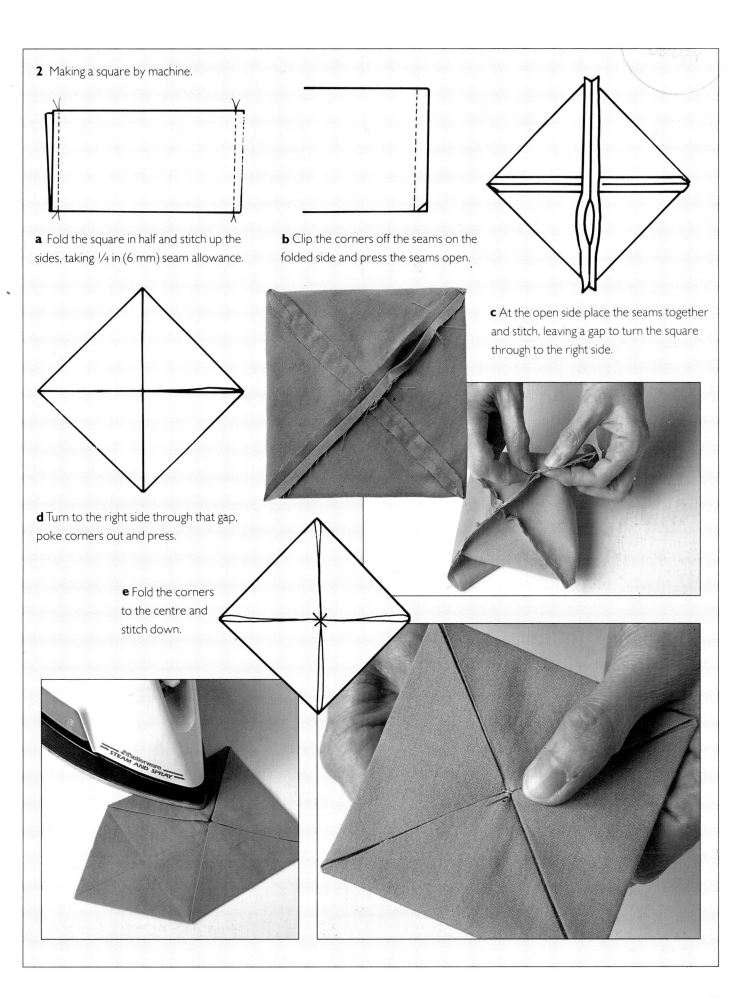

a Fold the square in half and stitch up the sides, taking ¼ in (6 mm) seam allowance.

b Clip the corners off the seams on the folded side and press the seams open.

c At the open side place the seams together and stitch, leaving a gap to turn the square through to the right side.

d Turn to the right side through that gap, poke corners out and press.

e Fold the corners to the centre and stitch down.

3 Sewing in the panel and making the pin-cushion.

Sew in the decorative panel.

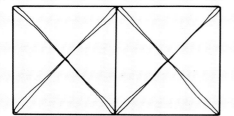

Stitch two prepared squares together.

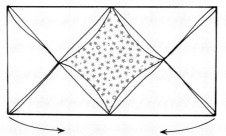

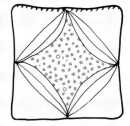

Fold the sides to centre back to form a tube and oversew right sides together. Then sew in the second decorative panel across the seam.

Stitch across top and bottom. Stuff firmly before closing the gap.

4 How to join squares together.

Four squares joined, seen from the right side.

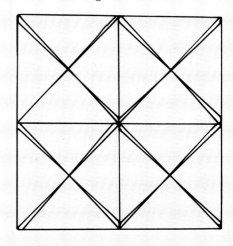

Prepare a number of squares. When you have enough, place them right sides together and join along one edge with whip-stitch from corner to corner.

Join as many squares as you need for your design.

Decorative panel using the cathedral window technique in silk, satin and taffeta.

5 Inserting the panels into the squares.

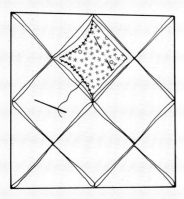

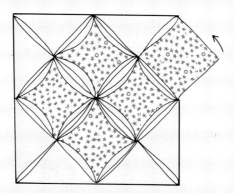

Measure the space between two of the background squares and cut pieces of decorative fabric in that size. Turn the folded edge of the background onto the decorative squares and hem down neatly.

At the edges, hem the backing down to two sides of the decorative square and fold the remaining half over to the back. Neaten the edges and hem down.

GLOSSARY

Appliqué The decorative technique of cutting out pieces of material and stitching them to a foundation.

Backing The piece of fabric used on the underside of a quilt.

Baste or Tack Temporary stitches to hold fabric in place until smaller, more secure stitching is done. In English patchwork, basting (tacking) stitches are also used to hold papers in fabric until shapes are stitched together. Large running stitches that can be easily removed should be used.

Batting or Wadding The insulating filler in a quilt.

Binding A strip of fabric stitched around the outer edges of the work, neatening and enclosing raw edges.

Block The design unit on which American patchwork is based. Blocks are usually geometric shapes which will fit into a grid and are repeated to form a complex overall design. Blocks are usually square but also come in other shapes.

Grain The way threads lie in woven fabric. Straight grain runs parallel to the selvedge and has the least amount of stretch. Cross grain runs from selvedge to selvedge. Bias grain cuts across the fabric diagonally and has the most stretch.

Patchwork The process of making a large piece of fabric from smaller ones. This can be done either by seaming pieces together or by sewing one fabric to another.

Piecing The sewing together of small pieces of fabric to form a larger whole piece.

Quilt A sandwich made from three layers of fabric consisting of the top (often decorative patchwork), the insulating filler and the backing.

Quilting Running stitches which hold the three layers of the quilt together. These can be done by hand or machine.

Raw Edge The unfinished edge of a fabric.

Selvedge The finished edges of a piece of fabric running the length of the fabric along either side.

Template The pattern from which patchwork shapes are cut. They are made of stiff material such as card, plastic or metal.

INDEX